ORGANIZATIONAL BUYING BEHAVIOR

Thomas V. Bonoma

Gerald Zaltman

AMERICAN
MARKETING
ASSOCIATION

Proceedings Series

ORGANIZATIONAL BUYING BEHAVIOR 3∂

Edited by

Thomas V. Bonoma
University of Pittsburgh

Gerald Zaltman
University of Pittsburgh

AMERICAN
MARKETING
ASSOCIATION

222 So. Riverside Plaza · Chicago, Illinois 60606 · (312) 648-0536

Printed in the United States of America

Cover design by Mary Jo Galluppi

Library of Congress Cataloging in Publication Data
Main entry under title:

Organizational buying behavior.

Papers of a workshop sponsored by the American
Marketing Association and the Graduate School of
Business, University of Pittsburgh and held at the
University of Pittsburgh, April, 1976.
Bibliography: p.
1. Purchasing--Congresses. 2. Industrial procure-
ment--Congresses. 3. Organizational behavior--
Congresses. I. Bonoma, Thomas V. II. Zaltman, Gerald.
III. American Marketing Association. IV. Pittsburgh.
University. Graduate School of Business.
HF5437.07   658.7'2   77-27509
ISBN 0-87757-106-6

TABLE OF CONTENTS

TABLE OF CONTENTS

INTRODUCTION

This report is the product of a two-day workshop on organizational buying behavior held in April, 1976 at the University of Pittsburgh. The workshop was co-sponsored by the American Marketing Association and the Graduate School of Business, University of Pittsburgh. This book is divided into two major sections. The first is this overview of organizational buying behavior. It is the editors' summary of verbatim transcripts compiled during two days of discussions by workshop participants. The balance of this proceedings presents original papers either submitted prior to the workshop by participants to stimulate discussion, or written after the workshop was completed.

The workshop was organized around a reconceptualization and classification of organizational buying behavior offered by Zaltman and Bonoma [173]. This classification is discussed at length below. Generally, a discussion revolved around one of four central topics in organizational buying: the purchasing agent; the buying center; professionalism and community among purchasers; and organizational and environmental effects on the buying process. Participants were asked to target their presentation on one of these four major areas.

WORKSHOP PROCESS

Introduction to the Transcripts: The Organizational Buying Locus of Influences Grid

The format for the workshop was provided by the social influence conceptualization of organizational buying behavior offered by Bonoma and Zaltman, which is shown in Fig. 1.

The Organizational Buying Locus of Influence classification is drawn from the transactional bases of social psychology. It recognizes, first and foremost, that the organizational buying process is

1

FIGURE 1

The Organizational Buying Locus of Influences Grid

ORGANIZATIONAL LOCUS

	Within the Organization	Between Organizations
	I. Intradepartmental, Intra-organizational Influences	III. Intradepartmental, Intra-organizational Influences
Within Purchasing Department	**THE P.A.: FACTORS IN BUYING** • Social factors • Decision strategies • Price, cost factors • Product type and stage • Reinvention • Supply continuity and shortage • Computerization • Bidding, rating systems • Risk avoidance • Promotion	**PROFESSIONALISM AMONG PURCHASERS** • Face-to-face communication satisfaction • Trade shows and press • Rising status • Reciprocity I
	II. Interdepartmental, Intra-organizational Influences	IV. Interdepartmental Inter-organizational Influences
Between Departments	**THE BUYING CENTER** • Organizational structure • Power and conflict processes • Gatekeeper role • Role theory • Climate • Hierarchically imposed buying; interlocking factors • Information scanning	**ORGANIZATIONS AND ENVIRONMENT** • Technological changes • Nature of suppliers • Nature of business • Cooperative buying • Governmental influences • Legalities • Reciprocity II

Note: Large-type labels indicate general concept areas. Small-type headings indicate specific topics addressed in workshop discussions. Hence, the subheads are not exhaustive of the generic concepts.

an interactive, dyadic, and transactional process. In this view, inter-active social factors are presumed to be dominant influences on the organizational buying process. In other words, it is improper and theoretically impossible to speak of organizational buying without also speaking of organizational selling. It is theoretically impossible to speak of purchasing agents as "independent" agents, since they are affected by colleagues within the organization as well as those with whom they interact outside the organization.

Thus, the problem in understanding organizational buying be-havior is seen by the Bonoma-Zaltman conceptualization as a prob-lem in identifying the social influences exerted from various sources on purchasers.

The rows of Fig. 1 show that there is a departmental, locus of influence which recognizes the notion of the "buying center." That is, the influences to which purchasing managers (for example) may be subjected include those emanating from their own depart-ment, as well as those emanating from other departments making up the organization. Secondly, the columns of Fig. 1 show that there is an organizational or "corporate" locus of influence. Social in-fluences impinging on purchasing managers may emanate from within their own organization or may arise from the outside. The combination of each of these influence sources produces the four-fold figure represented in the diagram.

Cell 1 of the grid, the Intradepartmental, Intraorganizational In-fluences cell, concerns factors internal to the purchasing agent or the buying center. A very substantial portion of the previous litera-ture on industrial buying processes pertains to this cell.

Cell 2, the Interdepartmental, Intraorganizational Influences cell, pertains largely to the buying center as it operates internally and as it relates to the other departments within the organization. Examples of concerns treated in this cell are the gatekeeper role served by members of the buying center, the conflicts characterizing the buying center's relationship to other departments with factional interests in the purchasing process (design, production), and the overall organizational structure as it facilitates or inhibits buying. Fig. 1 lists the major issues identified by workshop participants as falling into Cell 2. They are discussed at greater length below.

3

Cell 3, the Intradepartmental, Interorganizational Influences cell, concerns itself with interfirm or environmental factors as these affect the purchasing department or group. This cell lists influences such as professional and trade associations on purchasing managers and others involved in purchasing. The role of trade shows and the trade press in the purchasing process, the role of face-to-face communication, and organizational intelligence activities (including illegal reciprocity) were identified and discussed by workshop participants under Cell 3.

Cell 4, the Interdepartmental, Interorganizational Influences cell, focuses attention on the opportunities and constraints posed both by other firms (customers and competitors) and by government agencies. Although relatively little information exists about the impact of these environmental factors on relationships among groups within a firm, workshop participants were able to vouch for their importance.

In the sections to follow, topics discussed during the workshop are organized roughly according to the four cells in Fig. 1. This simply facilitates their presentation. In reality, few phenomena fall exclusively into one or another cell.

Intradepartmental, Intraorganizational Influences

Social Factors in the Buying Process.

Three major issues came to light in workshop discussions into the determinants of the buying decision. Their order of importance in the buying process, according to workshop participants, are (1) the attraction of the buyer for the seller or selling firm, (2) the buyer's evaluation of the selling firm's reputation, and (3) the buyer's own status or power position within the purchasing department.

The friendships maintained by purchasing agents are important but are very often ignored, or even denied, in traditional treatments. Although this does not mean that decisions by purchasing managers are not based on competitive bidding, it does imply that the purchasing agent may work diligently with a friend to "get him com-

4

petitive." Such a relationship may involve specifications which uniquely relate to the friend or giving a friend the "undertaker's look" at the price at which a bid will be given to a competitor in order to see if the friend can meet it.

Tailoring specifications may also be done for professional reasons, of course, and this is where evaluation of a selling firm's reputation becomes important. It may be thought that one firm might be particularly well-suited to perform a supply task because of size or history. Also a purchasing organization needs to deal with a selling organization which they know will be around in the future, especially if a large capital outlay is involved. For example, in purchasing capital equipment which is expected to last for a number of years, there is a strong preference for a reliable, stable, and financially sound supplier who will be readily available when replacement parts are needed.

The purchasing manager's relationship to others within the purchasing organization is a third central influence in the buying process. A strong and dominant purchasing manager, for example, will be expected to exert a disproportionate influence over conflicting opinions regarding a potential purchase. Weak or ineffectual purchasing managers will be unable to negotiate hard-line bargains and other favorable terms for their organization.

These three factors—attraction, reputational issues, and personality or power of the purchasing manager—require further research, as does the entire issue of the interpersonal relationships maintained by purchasing managers. To the best of our knowledge, it is fair to state that these social factors operate to a far greater degree than more traditionally studied purchasing factors such as computerization, price and cost.

Decision Strategies

When studying the purchase act itself, it is common to apply any one of a number of rational decision models. Cost-minimization and vendor rating systems are examples of the many rational decision models employed to study this process. However, it was the opinion of a substantial number of workshop participants that such models, which do not reflect the importance of social factors, are less than satisfactory in accounting for the buying act.

They proposed a number of alternate, and possibly preferable, ways of studying the organizational buying process at the level of the individual purchasing manager. Among them were the conflict and social influence models of Bonoma and his colleagues, social judgment models in which comparisons are made to account for a particular purchase judgment, and other interactive models published in the literature of social psychology. The interested reader will find a much more detailed account of these models in Bagozzi's paper which is a part of this report.

Price and Cost Factors in the Purchasing Agent's Decision

The influence of price and cost factors in the purchasing agent's evaluation of bids or alternate sources of supply was a recurrent theme throughout the workshop. Three major viewpoints were expressed: (1) Price and cost factors are not as salient, or do not account for as much of the variance in the purchasing agent's decision, as social factors. (2) Price and cost factors in the organizational purchasing decision do have the primary influence ascribed to them traditionally in the literature, though sometimes without the knowledge and awareness, or at least the admission, of those doing the purchasing. And, (3) price and cost factors vary significantly according to the type of product or service acquired and the nature of the purchasing agent as well as other miscellaneous factors.

Regarding the first point, one of our participants presented empirical data strongly supporting the point that price and cost factors are not the central mechanisms in purchasing decisions. His data suggest that the successful bidder in a competitive bidding situation was the low bidder in only 40% of the cases and that "the salesman should not worry about the fact that he doesn't have a low price if he can sell on some other basis."

The second position suggests that price and cash factors are the central (or at least *a* central) predictor of organizational purchasing behavior, but that for social or interpersonal reasons purchasing agents will not admit their importance. As one participant put it, "There is almost an aversion to the question of price among the [purchasing] fraternity." In this view, it is seen as "bad taste" to admit that price is a central factor in supplier choice.

The third position suggests that there is such a difference in the importance of price and cost factors according to product or services line, the type of organization doing the purchasing, and the purchasing agent himself, that it is futile to generalize.

A significant minority of the participants felt that not many generalizations could or should be offered at this time. Again, in the words of one of our participants, "What we really need to do is to customize each sales presentation to fit the needs of that company. If it is an economizing firm, we have to go in with the low price. If it is a status firm, we have to do the kinds of things that make our firm a high status firm."

Product Type and Stage, Reinvention

The type of product or service acquired by the purchasing organization, as well as the product life cycle, received considerable attention by participants. The Robinson, Faris, and Wind New Task, Modified Rebuy, and Straight Rebuy model was such a theoretical mechanism most useful for predicting the importance of price, the decision strategy employed and risk avoidance. For example, as we move from a first time acquisition to repeat buying, the issues of price and cost predominate. Similarly, the purchasing agent's involvement in the purchase itself declines the more a product or service represents a new task item.

Berenson's product life cycle concept was examined empirically by Rink (see below), and was found to be supported by purchasing agents' responses. Workshop participants strongly endorsed the notion that the stage in the life cycle of a product or service (e.g., introduction versus maturity) is a second powerful influence on the purchasing agent's purchase deliberations. For example, larger more established firms may shy away altogether from new products or services in the introduction phase of the product life cycle.

A third critical product issue concerned re-invention. Re-invention is the process of adapting a product or service to fit the firm's unique needs. While re-invention is important at the implementation stage, it is also important at the initial purchase stage when the decision is made to acquire or not acquire a given product. The conditions under which re-invention is an important factor need to be clarified. This is an important issue and models of industrial buying should reflect the possibility of product or service modification by the acquiring firm.

Supply Continuity and Shortages

Perhaps as a result of the 1974-75 supplier shortages, the notion of supply continuity was raised throughout the workshop as a predictor of individual purchase decisions. Where quality, price, and risk levels are taken as givens, supply continuity in a time of shortage, or even in a time of plenty when shortages are anticipated, may be the central factor in the buying decision.

It should be noted, however, that the selling firm has interesting ways of responding to this problem. Making bids on a product or service for which the selling firm knows it cannot meet specifications is one standard way of keeping one's name in front of the buyer, and at the same time implying a continuity of relationship which may not be attainable, but which nonetheless influences future purchasing decisions.

A clear principle which emerged from the discussions was that the greater the number of alternate suppliers, the lower the general concern with continuity of supply in any purchase decision.

Computerization, Bidding, and Vendor Rating Systems

The role of computerization in the purchasing function was not seen as a revolutionary tool, but rather as a technique permitting intelligent evaluation of bits of vendor information, as well as removing much of the drudgery from the purchase of rebuys and maintenance equipment.

The computer is especially useful in rebuy situations, where considerations of ultimate cost, rather than immediate cost, are paramount. The addition of computerized decision-making capabilities—where a computer program can be written to simplify comparative vendor evaluation, inventory updating, and automatic reordering of certain items—not only takes much of the lower level work from the purchasing agent's desk, but often permits a more thorough evaluation of possible vendors. Materials management systems, where the purchasing department orders and follows up on all materials and inventories, were not felt by participants to provide a very realistic picture of the purchasing manager's role.

Computerization is really a special subtopic of the subject of vendor evaluation. Vendor evaluation is a matter of immediate concern in the purchasing process. How should vendors be evaluated, and what constitutes a reasonably exhaustive and sufficient set of attributes against which to measure their services? Although one can generate endless lists of customer service variables, delivery time variables, and stock-out ratios, one of the best mechanisms for vendor evaluation may be publicizing those suppliers who *do not* meet organizational requirements. One buying organization draws up a list each month of its "ten worst suppliers" and posts it in public view in the corporate offices. The company reports that firms so listed quickly take effective remedial action.

The true competitiveness of competitive bidding has already been discussed. The competitive bidding process is often a cover for less than competitive buying practices, and probably should generally be regarded as such. Further, competitive bidding, especially in highly technological or specialized buying situations, is sometimes neither appropriate nor useful for the vendor or the buying organization.

One empirical study of bid tabs (key criteria recorded from competitive bids for various potential suppliers) found that (1) low price was not a key to successful bidding; (2) a number of submitted bids did not, and apparently were not intended to, meet public specifications, but served more social or publicity purposes; and (3) social importance or status (as indicated above) was more frequently associated with successful bidding than were normal vendor rating factors such as delivery time.

9

Risk and Risk Avoidance

One of the most frequently named factors in the individual purchase decision was that of risk, or, more appropriately, risk avoidance. It was generally assumed that purchasing agents strive to minimize the risks (social and fiscal) associated with the acquisition of a new product or service. Secondary data sources such as Dun and Bradstreet are most often used as initial risk minimization strategies. The company not listed in such sources is often not regarded as so viable an alternative as one which is. For important potential suppliers, such factors as the unionization of factories, who has the money behind a given firm, and other factors ostensibly unrelated to the purchase decision may be seriously evaluated in terms of the degree of risk implicit in purchasing from that supplier. Generally, the more risk involved in the decision, the deeper you probe.

Social factors, such as those cited above, may act to reduce risk, even when more objective criteria give unfavorable results. Trusting or liking the seller, or having good reports about him, all act to reduce risk to manageable levels even in new task purchasing situations. Experience and expertise, other social factors, are also very important where risk is high. Not surprisingly, reliability, which often translates into size of the potential supplying firm, is used as a primary index of the degree of risk associated with the purchase. IBM typewriters, for example, are evaluated somewhat differently than Olivetti equipment on the risk variable. As one participant said, the smaller suppliers "may be great guys, but I can't afford the risk exposure."

Conclusions and Implications

Cell 1 of the Organizational Buying Locus of Influences Grid—the Intradepartmental, Intraorganizational Influences cell—addresses relationships among individuals as these affect the buying process. Whether decision strategies are rational or irrational is unclear. However, the predominance of social factors and risk avoidance in the buying process would suggest that the latter is probably the more correct.

How buying decisions are made varies with product type and product life cycle stage. Price and cost factors may or may not match with their traditionally assumed importance levels in the purchase decision, and certainly do not do so across the board.

Supply continuity in times of shortage appears to be another influential, but largely unstudied, predictor of purchasing decisions. And vendor bidder and rating systems appear to be in need of substantial re-thinking so that they will allow for the presence of social factors in the buyer/seller relationship.

Interdepartmental, Intraorganizational Influences

Cell 2 is concerned largely with the structure and function of the Webster and Wind concept of the buying center, or that aggregation of individuals involved in the various stages of any one purchase decision. Workshop participants discussed several important facets of the buying center which are summarized below.

The Nature of the Buying Center

Considerable research is needed to evaluate a number of key issues involved in the idea of a buying center. First of all, what individuals representing what departments usually make up a buying center? Is such a question even meaningful? Is there a general pattern to the membership of buying centers in organizations? Why, and how, do different members of a buying center make different judgments regarding a product or service acquisition? How are these judgments integrated?

For example, an accountant, a financial officer, an engineer, a metallurgical scientist, and a production vice president might evaluate the different attributes of a single piece of equipment quite differently. Depending upon the kind of company, some of these individuals would not even be included in the buying decision. The research necessary to answer such questions as those above has not been conducted to date, rendering the concept of the buying center much less useful as a hypothetical construct. In short, we do not know at this time how buying centers are composed, who tends to

11

participate in them, nor how decisions are made by the participating individuals. Though the concept of the buying center is a necessary and extremely fruitful innovation, it is nonetheless one that needs to be moved from its purely theoretical status to one which can be actively utilized by the management scientist and the practicing manager alike.

Issues of Organizational Structure

Some companies want only a purchasing operation that serves all other parts of the company in a clerical capacity. That is, the purchasing group assumes the responsibility only for paper work, while others in the firm make functional buying decisions. Other companies want a purchasing department made up of technically trained people who can combat fixed or rigid ideas held elsewhere in the firm, and who can contribute to the technical as well as the marketing and business aspects of purchasing.

Why do some firms prefer weak departments in lieu of strong ones, and vice versa? Under what conditions is a strong department better or worse than a weak one? Such questions are among the major ones relating the structure of the buying center to company success.

The general feeling, endorsed by all workshop participants, was that the buying center is "a messy animal," one which may necessitate radically different methodologies for meaningful empirical study. Most of the end results of a purchasing organization are really a compromise between what one would like to do and what one can effectively accomplish.

One must take into consideration the fact that the purchasing organization is so structured in order to maximize purchasing clout, to bring the maximum impact to the market in which one is dealing. Each unit within one's own company is serving its own interests. Each would like to have the purchasing organization be totally in accordance with its own individual interests. Given a number of these factional and mutually exclusive demands, purchasing is required to pool the different requirements across division lines

12

and present a single-faced entity in order to deal with the supplier marketplace.

In the course of examining the phenomenon of the buying center, two contradictory lines of thought emerged from the workshop. The first was that more careful application of conflict theory must be applied to empirical studies of the purchasing act. The second was, as one participant put it, "we are paying too much attention to the kind of formal organization design offered by management scientists, and it really doesn't make too much difference because most of the decisions are being made by informal coalitions."

The first approach suggests a more sociological analysis of the buying center; the second suggests that, since organizational structure may be irrelevant to ultimate purchasing acts, one should focus primarily on the individual purchasing manager or other relevant factor in order to understand organizational buying behavior. Our opinion is that the former view is the more fruitful approach.

Power in the Buying Center

The bases for power in the buying center vary. If one member of the buying center, say an engineer, makes decisions that affect another member's paycheck and promotions, then at least two people will consider engineering factors to be very important in the purchase evaluation. Much work needs to be done to identify the kinds of power exercised and the basis of power employed in a buying center. Insights gained from studies of the social psychology of conflict could be extremely helpful in designing and studying buying centers.

Hospital decision-making may be seen as an especially illuminating example of the buying center concept—as well as the power base—at work. The buying decision in hospital acquisitions, especially of the modified rebuy variety, often involves a hospital administrator, a physician, and a nurse. Interestingly, when such situations are studied closely, the nurses often are found to exert final purchasing authority with regard to office equipment, supplies, and other rebuy items, even including the somewhat substantial purchase of medical treatment apparatus. This is because the administrator does not have the knowledge or expertise to make such decisions, the physician does not have the time, and the nurse has a modicum of both. The administrator, charged with formal purchasing authority in the hospital organization, may primarily serve in the role of an information gatekeeper to make others in the organization aware of new purchase possibilities, a topic to which we now turn.

The Gatekeeper Role in the Buying Center

It is very important for the student of industrial marketing to understand the role of gatekeepers. Gatekeepers filter information as it flows between a source and its ultimate destination. Gatekeepers can, in effect, become decision makers by allowing more of the favorable information from a formal bidder to flow to formal decision makers. Gatekeepers may not always be aware that they are performing this function.

Purchasing managers or, more correctly, those persons involved in a functional buying center, may be in excellent positions to serve as gatekeepers for their firms. By being "closest to the action," the purchasing manager may filter information from bidding firms in such a manner that the final outcome of the purchase can be controlled in accordance with the purchasing manager's biases.

Additionally, the industrial salesman or other supplier's representative may have to take on added roles in order to insure that the information presented will be transmitted along proper channels. Cases were reported of salesmen having to play Monopoly or engage in similar time-consuming activities for hours on end in order to be allowed the privilege of presenting a bid which had a chance of being evaluated favorably by the purchasing manager.

When an organizational sub-unit, such as the buying center, is characterized by social conflict, status issues, and power jockeying, the role of the gatekeeper becomes especially critical. Gatekeepers can make sure that the benefits of a favored proposal are presented in a cost-saving light to the accountants, that the engineering innovations are emphasized to the engineers, and that the user benefits are emphasized to potential users in a manner which may predetermine the outcome of the purchasing decision.

There is a second manner in which members of the buying center in general, and the purchasing manager in particular, are especially likely to be good candidates as gatekeepers. It is in the idea of "the strength of weak ties." This refers to a pattern of membership in a wide variety of professional or social organizations which may serve as information sources for the member. A person who is weakly tied to many social groups stands an excellent chance of being among the first to be informed about a new product or service innovation, and, thus, of passing along this information to relevant individuals.

The members of a buying center would be expected to differ in the strengths of their weak ties according to their disciplinary identifications. Accountants, engineers, and other professionals probably would not be high in this variable, while individuals such as marketers and purchasing managers probably would be high. These latter then may possess some additional advantages as gatekeepers.

Organizational Climate and the Buying Center

As expressed by one of the participants, "The concept of organizational climate is a very vague one. It's one of the concepts in organization theory that, if you ask four people, they will give you eight answers." Here, we use the concept of organizational climate to talk about the support within the buying center for individual members as well as the communication processes taking place between the members of the buying center. Generally, organizational climate differences have not proved to be effective predictors of differences in buying patterns, decision strategies, or effectiveness. However, it may be that the problem is a simple one of definition and conceptualization and not of the irrelevance of the concept. In areas other than industrial marketing, most notably education, research has suggested that the acquisition of new educational services was directly related to changes introduced into the organizational climate.

The ideal climate for effective information scanning, new product or service innovation, and ultimate decision making appears to be a very decentralized, heterogeneous "project team" purchasing organization with little bureaucracy. Conflict is often encouraged rather than discouraged in such an environment, and consensus and cooperation are the primary decision mechanisms as opposed to hierarchical authority.

But the basic question still arises as to how effective would a purchasing organization based on such a design be, as compared to the linear, highly bureaucratized organizations employed in most profit firms. If the data from non-industrial marketing situations can be generalized, such a system could be implemented under extremely tight cost constraints at approximately the same expense currently being incurred by organizations for their existing purchasing organization.

At the present time, however, such recommendations are most useful only for the new task situation. The modified rebuy or habitual rebuys in which most firms engage with greatest frequency may be little affected by such organizational redesigns or changes in climate.

Hierarchically Imposed Buying: Interlocking Factors

Although there are rare exceptions, it is usually the case that upper management will neither dictate nor interfere with the purchasing function as performed by the buying center. Although the question must be raised in the course of an inquiry into organizational buyer behavior, it is the current opinion that such processes will not be found very significant in predicting the outcome of either major or minor purchases.

Summary and Conclusions: Cell 2

The state of knowledge concerning the buying center presents a contradiction. On the one hand, we have the theoretically relevant and substantively innovative concept of the buying center. This concept is a dynamic one which parallels the reality of purchasing organizations more correctly than an approach recommending the study of just the purchasing department or purchasing manager. On the other hand, we have no data regarding the nature of buying centers. For example, we have no information as to the individuals likely to be included in or excluded from buying decisions under various product or service classifications, and we have little information about how the individuals making up the buying center integrate their decision processes.

There are some hints, however, from the sociological and psychological literature which may some day go a long way toward illuminating the functions of the buying center. Conflict processes, power relationships, and other variables would all seem to be, on an *a priori* basis, important factors in purchasing decisions.

Who has the power? What factional interests are being advanced for future consideration? What organizational constraints are present or absent? What role relationships exist among the members of a buying center? All these are important concerns for the theorist or researcher who would apply his expertise to organizational buyer behavior.

A second potentially productive inroad may be made through the concepts of information scanning and the gatekeeper role. Because of his or her unique status in purchasing—whether it is formally as a purchasing manager or informally as a frequently consulted member of the buying center—the "buyer" in an organization often has access to information not available to others. Consequently, he or she may make the decision to either pass on this information in a favorable or unfavorable light, or to suppress it. In this manner, even though ultimate authority does not rest with the gatekeeper, the outcome of purchasing decisions may be determined at this level.

Finally, though mentioned as important factors, neither organizational climate nor the phenomenon of hierarchically imposed buying strategies seems to be central to understanding the buying center or its operation, except under certain restricted circumstances.

Intradepartmental, Interorganizational Influences

The concept of interfirm factors as they affect the purchasing group is a new one in the organizational buying behavior literature. Cell 3 suggests that communicational, promotional and related media affect the relationships of purchasing agents with their colleagues in other firms and exert strong influences on the organizational purchasing process.

More specifically, the effects of face-to-face communications within an industry or buying group, the functions of trade shows and the trade press, formal or informal organizational intelligence activities, and certain legal transactions are addressed here.

Face-to-Face Communications

The importance of purchase-related word-of-mouth communication among buying firms is greatly underestimated. Whether this information is gathered over the phone, at trade shows and various professional meetings, or through other sources is inconsequential. In general, little is known in a systematic fashion about informal communication with respect to purchasing decisions. Research is needed to indicate how information seeking and processing of this sort varies by industry, personnel involved, type of purchase, or type of information.

The existing literature indicates that:

1. Technology transfers especially occur through face-to-face communications between scientific and technical personnel. It is ordinarily the highly mobile, upper level executives rather than the purchasing managers who acquire the information necessary for purchase and make the ultimate decision.
2. One of the implicit purposes of trade shows is to serve as a gathering place where such face-to-face communications can be accomplished. Actually, trade show travel may be under-budgeted due to a general underestimation of the importance of such interpersonal contacts outside the firm.
3. Another source of information transfer in face-to-face communications is the outside consultant, who may bring with him new information or new ways of thinking. In addition, newly hired purchasing managers or other executives bring new ideas and may also be excellent sources of information about new products or services.

18

The major communication network within purchasing, however, is within purchasing groups that reach across firms in the same industry. One purchasing manager knows who is interested in the same petro-chemicals or the same kinds of equipment as he is and he doesn't hesitate to draw on their experience with companies concerning opinions, price trends, or market trends.

The second major source of information for purchasing managers is the marketing or sales staffs of various vendors. As one participant put it, "You may never give him an order but you always give him an interview because he is helping you, and you also get the other side of the fence from your associates in the buying end and you melt these two together and balance them."

Thus, it appears that, in addition to the sources identified above, the bulk of face-to-face communications involving the purchasing group is either characterized by groups of purchasers within the same industry or occurs between purchasers and potential vendors.

Trade Shows and Journals

The importance of the trade show as a place for face-to-face communication between purchasers has been noted above. However, trade shows and the trade press serve a second function in establishing communication among purchasers, that of a promotional or advertising nature. What little literature there is on evaluation of industrial advertising, whether occurring at a trade show or in the trade press, seems to suggest that considerable industrial advertising is misdirected. That is, it is not necessarily directed to the individual having the greatest influence in the buying process, hence it tends to stress the wrong product attributes.

In the case of advertising which is being directed to a purchasing manager, one analysis of such material indicates that the technical elements of the product are stressed, rather than cost savings or delivery capability, factors which the purchasing manager would be expected to consider in his overall evaluation of a product or service.

Some further support for this conclusion was provided by analysis performed four years ago of approximately one hundred products in the purchasing journals directed to chemists and research and development personnel. Approximately 80 percent of the ads analyzed were found to be identical, whether directed toward chemists or R&D people. The clear implication is that many industrial marketers simply developed one ad and submitted it to magazines directed toward two very different audiences.

In general, little is known about industrial advertising. What is known suggests that much of it may not employ even rudimentary marketing concepts of segmentation, may not be targeted specifically to different audiences, and may generally be ineffective.

The Rising Status of Purchasing Management

Available data, including a survey of trade journals, indicate that the purchasing manager is clearly in a period of rising professional status. Major reasons for the increased importance of the purchasing professional are the recent material shortages and the current lack of rapidly growing markets. Consequently, companies have to monitor their income and costs much more closely to keep their profit margins satisfactory. Such concerns tend to highlight the purchasing professional as a cost conscious trouble shooter who can effectively contribute to resolving these tough organizational problems.

To the extent that there is a rise in the status of purchasing professionals and an increase in their sense of professionalism, we may expect an increase in the importance of face-to-face communication at professional meetings and trade shows, as well as an increased use of the trade press. Consequently, the lack of empirical literature evaluating the importance of this new status is disturbing. It remains an urgent matter for increased study.

Reciprocity I: Supplier-Purchaser Reciprocity

The issues of formal and informal reciprocity at the supplier-purchaser level have been commented on at some length in the literature. However, much of the commentary is speculative, and reciprocity has received little or no empirical study because of its sensitive nature. There is, however, little question among those who do purchasing that reciprocity is a fact of life, whether of the formal "You buy from me and I will buy from you," sort or of the more informal type springing from such seemingly innocent activities as luncheon dates, gifts, and other "sales promotions."

Workshop participants all agreed that the subject of industrial reciprocity should be given immediate and lengthy study to determine its parameters and, more importantly, its effects on industrial marketing in general and the industrial buying process in particular. Undoubtedly, methods will have to be developed to match the sensitive nature of this phenomenon.

Conclusion: Cell 3

It is clear that intradepartmental and interorganizational influences have not been a matter or major concern to industrial marketers, nor to students of organizational buying behavior. Face-to-face communication especially is an important but relatively unstudied phenomenon in the buying process. Trade shows and journals are viewed as important sources of community feeling and common information among professional purchasers. These media need to be subjected to strict empirical scrutiny. The rising status and increased sense of professionalism among purchasing managers seems well documented, and only heightens their importance as a factor in industrial buying behavior. Finally, the "sins" of purchasing transactions, reciprocity both formal and informal, need to be studied in a less speculative light as they have inescapable relationships to feelings of attraction and friendship, and hence to the purchasing decision itself.

Interdepartmental, Interorganizational Influences

Cell 4 focuses our attention on Interdepartmental, Interorganization Influences. This cell concerns itself with environmental opportunities and constraints on the buying center posed by other firms (both customers and competitors) and government agencies. Although relatively little information exists regarding the impact of such factors on relationships among groups with respect to purchasing decisions, the workshop included commentary on technological changes, interfirm reciprocity issues, the nature of the supplier universe, the general tenor of business, the phenomenon of cooperative buying, and governmental influences.

Buying in an Era of Technological Change

Available evidence indicates a simple but strong empirical relationship: As the rate of technological change increases, the importance of the purchasing manager in the organizational acquisition process decreases. At the same time, the importance of technical and engineering individuals making up the buying center increases rapidly, and they may well become the sole, or at least major, authorizers of purchases.

In industries in which the rate of change is not a factor, the purchasing manager may increase in importance in the purchase authorization process. This finding has implications for the marketing of highly technological or scientific products or services as well as for the promotion of industrial products and services. It also implies the need for different marketing strategies in times of change versus times of stability. Thus, technological change functions much as price in predicting the purchasing manager's relative influence on the buying act. As price or technological change increases, the less important the purchasing manager is in purchase decisions.

The Nature of Suppliers and the Nature of the Business

Both the universe of suppliers available to potential purchasers and the specific objectives of the business in which they find themselves have important effects on organizational buying behavior. Regarding the first point, both the size of potential suppliers and the number of alternative suppliers appear to be critical factors. Large suppliers are evaluated on clearly different criteria from smaller ones, since the larger ones do not pose as many risks. Financial analyses of smaller suppliers may be deemed necessary whereas they are not performed on firms of greater size.

Similarly, the larger the number of alternative suppliers of a given product or service, the more probable it is that an order of a given size will be "spread around" among a number of different suppliers to assure supply continuity in case of crisis, changing environment, business failure, or other catastrophe. Firms may, and do, encourage supplier competition by upgrading their poorer suppliers with capital equipment paid for by the buyer, technical assistance and research collaboration.

All of these investments are viewed as sound purchasing management. It is a strategy of maintaining competition in the supplier marketplace in order not to find oneself in the position of being dictated to by one or a few vendors. The phenomenon of encouraging supplier competitiveness through purchaser investments needs to be scrutinized carefully since little or no data exists outside of case studies.

Strong evidence indicates that for-profit firms engage in purchasing activities very different from those organized on a not-for-profit basis. For example, one study shows that, when questioned about why a particular piece of capital equipment was purchased, only an insignificant fraction of purchasing managers in for-profit companies justified their purchase by suggesting they had a budget for its acquisition. Over one-quarter of the individuals in not-for-profit organizations used this reason as justification of their acquisition. This particular example is an instance of the generally known phenomenon of not-for-profit purchasing that, unless budgets are overspent in a given fiscal period, there is a better than even probability that they will be cut during the next fiscal period. The rationale for not-for-profit purchasing often is not so much fulfilling of need as it is a justification of future budgetary expansion. For-profit firms, though susceptible to the same disease, are not as likely to contract it as severely.

Cooperative Buying Practices

Running counter to the forces encouraging competition among vendors, there is increasing evidence of firms within the same industry or geographical area joining in "cooperative buying." The phenomenon has been most clearly seen in the hospital supply

23

industry to date, though it has long been a common practice in agri-business. Buying cooperatives, to the extent that they can successfully overcome the inevitable conflicts posed in such a coalition, offer a new model to be analyzed by the student of industrial marketing. The buyer, traditionally the weaker participant in the vendor-buyer combination, now exerts significant counter power, comparable to that of the largest manufacturers in some agri-business industries. In the more successful cooperatives, the distribution function is taken over as well, and sometimes transportation, customer service, and other operations traditionally performed by the selling company.

Though there is little data on buying cooperatives *per se*, group buying among otherwise competing firms may well become the model for the future because of the economies it affords. These economies are so great that the model is often irresistible, and the fact that it has so far been restricted largely to agriculture and the not-for-profit sector should not lull students of industrial marketing into thinking that it is not yet an appropriate matter for study and theoretical development.

Governmental and Legal Influences in Organizational Buying

One of the little studied effects of environmental change on a particular company is the impact of relationships between two or more other organizations in the same environment.

Federal government purchases, for example, sometimes include certain product specifications which may result in, let's say, less noise pollution. In some instances, noise is of minor concern in the particular application involved. However, the issue may be of concern to non-government users, and it may be the government's intent to change specifications in order to thereby ultimately improve the product.

One relatively unknown governmental program, the Experimental Technological Incentives Program (ETIP) is a concerted attempt by the federal procurement office to write product and service specifications in order to promote product development along the lines endorsed by federal policy. For example, certain specifications have been re-written for power lawn mowers such that, if a supplier wishes to sell to the federal government, his product must meet certain reduced noise tolerance levels. Since it is ordinarily impractical for a producer to make one product for the federal government and another for private consumption, the net effect is to encourage noise abatement devices on all lawn mowers. Similar tactics have been employed regarding safety standards and other federally desired, but commercially uneconomical, product modifications.

But one should not single out the federal government as the major influence here. The largest companies within any industry often exert exactly the same kind of influence on potential suppliers. When any company is in a position to consume all or most of the output of another company, one suspects that this kind of environmental pressure may exert a major influence on product modification.

Companies also operate within a legal environment and must be increasingly sensitive to the consequences of substandard product or service quality. Regardless of whether a firm markets to the industrial or end use sectors, it can be held liable for the quality of materials which reach the end use market. The result is that the purchasing manager often must balance projected failure rates and/or safety legislation (areas in which he or she may be very inexpert) against the company's own standards of production and design. The consequences of a failure to correctly balance such diverse and often conflicting requirements may be a costly and unnecessary law suit.

Reciprocity II: Organizational and Environmental Pressures

The web of informal influences among a group of companies within a business environment is believed to have major effects on organizational buying behavior. For example, a banker who is also a member of the board of directors of a purchasing firm, and who has close ties with someone in a potential supplier firm, may constitute an informal influence on the purchasing manager of the first company.

However, the available data from practicing purchasing managers suggests that such influences exert slight effect. Similarly, the situation of interlocking directorates mentioned above has not generally been found of great importance in explaining the organizational purchasing process.

Conclusion: Environmental Issues

If little is known about the professionalism and sense of community among purchasing agents, even less data is available on environmental issues. However, workshop participants were able to cite instances of the importance of (1) the relationship between the rates of technological change and the degree of influence of the purchasing manager, (2) the size of supplier firms and the number of them available, (3) the phenomenon of cooperative buying, and (4) governmental influences. Much work obviously remains to be done.

Methodological Issues and Other Considerations

Among the major problems addressed by workshop participants was the problem of the shifting, changing, and ill-defined organization of the buying center as it awaits attempts to define it. Participants were also interested in problems raised by the interface of normal methods of marketing and the buying center's operations; and problems of researching the buying center concept in ways which would allow effective market segmentation of such organizations for further study.

Other considerations were raised. The first was the relationship of organizational buying behavior and the end use, or consumer, segment of the market. The second was the problem of whether and when to generalize when certain facts or relationships were found to apply to one particular company. The third was the problem of training new professionals entering industrial marketing, as well as providing incentives to encourage scholarship in this area.

A marketer, wanting to understand the behavior of buying or selling organizations, is faced with two basic choices in selecting a unit of analysis. One is to look mainly at the individual most frequently involved in the purchasing act. The other choice, and we believe it the more appropriate, is to start with an individual but to take into account all other relevant individuals within and outside the firm. Analyzing the individual in interactions with others, while the more meaningful, is also the more difficult.

There is thus a strong need for developing new methodologies in industrial marketing which will facilitate the study of buying centers as the units of analysis, rather than simply studying the individuals who compose them. A more complete description of this approach is presented in the Bonoma et al paper presented in Section II.

The Buying Organization

Another methodological problem facing organizational marketers is the fact that over a period of time different subgroups are involved in the buying process. One subgroup may be involved in defining the problem. Another may be charged with seeking solutions. Another may be primarily involved in adopting the decision, while still another subgroup is charged with the responsibility for implementation. These groups may involve very little overlap, may be difficult to define according to organization charts or other formal methods, and may change radically over time.

While it is easy to suggest that the individuals who overlap all of the shifting and changing subgroups may be the most influential in the entire process, industrial marketers are still faced with the basic problem of defining a buying center which is subject to changes in both its composition and its environment over time. The methods of sociology (most notably role-theory) and social psychology (most notably conflict and power analyses) appear to offer some solution to these problems, and at least represent a starting point for tighter empirical descriptions of buying activities in industrial marketing.

Segmenting Organizational Buying

An even larger problem is that of attempting to measure organizations in a way which would permit market segmentation. That is, given the clear relationships of organizational buying behavior *vis a vis* the buying center, the environment, and the sense of community among buyers, a much more fruitful path to classifying differences in industrial buying strategies may be to "segment" organizations rather than individual purchasing managers. Thus, one might expect differences between profit and not-for-profit organizations to reflect (a) different individuals involved in the buying process, (b) buying decisions made on different strategy grounds, and (c) differences in willingness to innovate or adapt new products and services to their needs.

One of the major problems in organizational buying behavior *per se* is simply that much descriptive work has not yet been done on a large scale. Investigators have preferred to send large sample surveys to a number of different purchasing managers in a large variety of firms, ignoring both the buying center concept and the fact that the buying process itself involves two parties—buyer and seller. A more fruitful research attack might be to study fewer organizations across more industries according to whatever intuitive classifications or segmentation strategies initially suggest themselves.

Marketing Methods and Organizational Buying Behavior

A serious methodological problem exists when intrafirm purchase decision are studied with the usual retrospective survey methods employed by marketers. Different people perceive the processes differently for any one of a number of reasons reviewed above, and may even report the processes in ways which differ from their actual perception due to their role position or other factors. Poor recall may account for some differences in perception, but conscious intent can be involved as well. Sometimes reported perceptions can be checked against written records, but often they cannot be. Basically, it is our contention that the retrospective survey methods employed by most marketers, in both the consumer and industrial areas, must be supplemented by other means when studying organizational buyer behavior. It may be necessary for researchers to actually place themselves in buying centers and to track decisions through their various stages in order to get some handle on the shifting sands of the buying center, outside influences, and myriad other factors.

Generalizing Research Findings on Organizational Buyer Behavior

Strong differences of opinion at the workshop centered on whether or not the findings on industrial marketing in general, and on organizational buying behavior in particular, can be applied to firms outside the industry under study. Several participants felt strongly that "It is difficult if not impossible to generalize findings in industrial marketing and buying activities."

The reasons for the negative opinion are clear. For one thing, buying centers are not the same in composition or strategy either across different industries or within one industry. Also, the composition of the buying center and buying strategies will be found to vary significantly by product class, type, size of the firm doing the buying, and size of the firm doing the selling.

A different opinion suggests that generalizations about organizational buying behavior may be possible in the future, but they must be generalizations of a very different sort than that to which we are accustomed in the area of consumer marketing. Such generalizing will, this view entails, involve segmenting companies rather than individuals in the organizational marketing sector. It will mean classifying from scratch and coupling a strong taxonomy of firms and industries with the variables which so far are known to account for differences in organizational buyer behavior. It will, finally, involve a strong infusion of those sciences best suited to dealing with shifting transactional analyses, namely, sociology and social psychology. Until these behavioral and transactionally-focused sciences are incorporated into marketing research, we reluctantly agree with the former group regarding the hope of generalizing industrial marketing findings. We do not, however, agree that generalizing will be impossible in the future. In fact, it is one solution likely to come about but only after a significant amount of further work has been completed.

Training and Support for Further Progress in Industrial Marketing

There is little support currently available to researchers who would study industrial marketing in general, or organizational

29

buyer behavior in particular. While scholarships and awards for such activities have existed in the past, they are currently in short supply, widely publicized, or otherwise hard to come by. The major marketing journals' emphasis on consumer, to the exclusion of industrial, marketing research is in a ratio of about five to one. This is another factor tending to discourage the brightest and best students in the latter category. Also there appear to be only a few professionals competent enough and willing to train students wishing to enter the field.

One of the most positive and easiest ways to remedy these difficulties is to get both AMA and non-AMA member firms to support training of graduate students in industrial marketing activities in general, and in organizational buying behavior in particular. Such an approach should go far beyond simply making data bases available for such students. It should include, at the very least, scholarships, cash awards, and willingness to take on students as full-time interns for periods up up to one year. It is only with the full and complete cooperation of industry that sufficient incentives will be created to attract the best and most capable students to study such important phenomena as organizational buying behavior.

DYADIC INTERACTIONS:
SOME CONCEPTUALIZATIONS

David T. Wilson
Professor of Marketing
Pennsylvania State University

Buyer-seller interaction reflects the organizational environment in which the interaction takes place. This report begins with a discussion of a decision process model of organizational buying as background to the discussion of buyer-seller interaction as an exchange process. The concepts presented here represent a gathering together of several of the author's papers that have explored the area of organizational buying behavior. Therefore, large sections of this report draw heavily upon previously published material, reflecting the attempt to synthesize several concepts into a more complete view of the dyadic buyer-seller process.

A DECISION PROCESS MODEL OF ORGANIZATIONAL BUYING

Lutz and Kakkar [89] make a strong plea for the inclusion of situational factors in the study of the interpersonal persuasion process. They present a model that "can be viewed as an intersection of three major classes of behavior theory: situational influence, decision process models, and social exchange theory" (p. 377). The decision process model presented here views the individual decision maker in the organizational buying center as an information processing unit. Perceptual bias, belief structures, perceived risk, decision style, and other intervening variables affect the central processing of information and the choice process.

Nevertheless, there are some significant differences between an individual acting for an organization and the same individual acting for himself. In addition to obvious organizational constraints, there is the fact that many problems are divided into subproblems [37, 98] and different individuals are assigned responsibility for each sub-problem. For example, quality problems may be assigned to engineering, delivery assigned to production, and terms of purchase to the purchasing department. Individuals are also highly trained to perform their tasks, which is not the usual consumer situation.

All these differences imply that the usual information processing and choice models need to be modified for use in organizational buying decisions.

The model detailed below is an attempt to synthesize other general models [147, 123, 110] into a series of propositions that can be empirically tested. A major addition to this model, with respect to previous models, is the incorporation of a powerful external memory [98] in the form of an EDP-supported purchasing system [159]. The importance of the external memory to an information processing system lies in the fact that "A problem solving program cannot be specified independently of its EM any more than it can be specified independently of its internal STM (Short Term Memory) and LTM (Long Term Memory). Hence, one can predict the problem solving program of an IPS (Individual Problem Solver) only after characterizing the EM's available to it" [98]. This decision process model is specified at a more macro level than the Newell and Simon model.

A basic tenet of this model is that individuals, not groups or organizations, process information and make choices. The individual within an organization is subjected to the influence of membership and referent groups as well as organization and environmental constraints, but this is still an individual level model. The complex definition of these situational factors is thoroughly summarized by Lutz and Kakkar [89] making further discussion unnecessary.

The term "decision process" is used as shorthand for the process that includes information-acquisition, processing activities, choice processes, and development of goals and other criteria used in choosing among alternatives [147].

32

Structure of the Model

The basic structure of the model is detailed in Fig. 1. The individual decision maker is the core of the model. Fig. 1 depicts two individuals representing the concept of the buying center. The actual size of the buying center is a function of the buying task and the organization. In other words, its size is situation specific.

Each individual has an information processing system, the input to which is filtered through a perceptual system [122]. The external

FIGURE 1

Structural Elements of the Decision Process Model

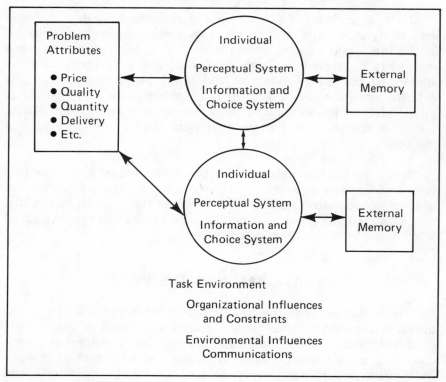

33

memory represents the notion that an organization buyer's information processing system is likely to be supported by some form of external memory ranging from a hand calculator to an on-line package of analytical programs.

The other important element in this basic structure is the conceptualization of the buying problem as a set of attributes representing the product and the vendor [150, 110, 82]. This is not a new concept, but it is an important one for this model. Attributes such as design of product, cost of application, performance life, and engineering help [150], along with the traditional attributes of price, quality, and delivery, make up the set of product-vendor attributes. This attribute set may be perceived differently by each member of the buying center in accordance with the individual's goals. Lehmann and O'Shaughnessy [82] suggest that the importance of separate individual attributes varies as a function of the buying situation.

The task environment in which the separate individual operates very likely shapes the importance of the specific individual attributes in the total product-vendor bundle. In Fig. 1, the task environment represents both environmental influences and organizational influences and constraints. Webster and Wind [147] characterize the external environment as a source of information which serves as input into the individual's decision making process. A great deal of this information is in the form of persuasive communications of marketers.

To review, the basic elements of the model are an individual in a task environment attempting to make a choice from a number of product-vendor attribute sets. This model is the simplest representation of a complex process. It can be used to describe simple (rebuy) or complex (new task) buying behavior.

OPERATIONALIZING THE MODEL

It is contended that the task environment is the specifier of the operationalization of the model. The type of buying task—rebuy, modified rebuy, or new task—and the structural properties of the corporate organization greatly influence the relationship between individuals within the buying center. In addition, Newell and

Simon [98] suggest that the task environment determines, to a large extent, the behavior of the individual. Their definition of task environment "refers to an environment coupled with a goal, problem, or task." They note the distinction between the demands of a task environment and the psychology of the subject. This model accepts this distinction without further amplification.

Given a task environment, the four relational concepts of quasi-resolution of conflict, uncertainty avoidance, problemistic search, and organizational learning [110, 38] suggest the forms that the model will assume as the buying task moves from a rebuy situation to a new task situation.

The Simple Case

In a straight rebuy situation, the buyer has a clear understanding of the importance of the attributes of the situation and knows which attributes are possessed by each product-vendor set. A decision rule (the exact nature of which is not the concern of this report) is applied, and a choice of vendor is made. This rebuy process can be relatively easily converted to a closed loop automatic purchasing process in which the buyer need only participate under the rule of management by exception [160] and only take over the control of the decision-making system when an abnormality exists.

It should be noted that a rebuy situation develops as the result of a new task situation. The four relational concepts have resulted in a stable rebuying situation as uncertainty has been reduced to acceptable levels and the coalition in the buying center has been satisfied.

A More Complex Case

The new task situation represents the other end of the scale. There are many product-vendor attribute sets to be evaluated. Uncertainty is high as to the actual possession of attributes by the individual product-vendor combination. As the complexity of the task increases, a larger buying center may be created to represent groups with conflicting goals and interests.

The model can be conceived as operating in the following manner: First, responsibility for separate attributes, within the bundle of product-vendor attributes, is assigned to individuals within the buying center, utilizing the rules of the quasi-resolution of conflict proposition. Organizational learning may be operative in that past experience may influence the current allocation of attributes to individuals. Also, the assignment of responsibility would likely reflect the nature of the task, the skills of the individual, and other organizational variables.

A complex task situation confronts the individuals in a buying center with a likely information overload. It is suggested that the buying center seeks to reduce the complexity of the task by the easiest means possible. Problemistic search of some sort following to the principle of "information processing parsimony" [57] is required to reduce the number of product-vendor sets under consideration. The actual methods that buying centers use can only be speculated and are beyond the scope of this report.

The focus of the report to this point has been on the individuals within the buying organization. The remainder will examine interaction between the buyer and the seller as a dyadic relationship. In reality, as the buying task increases in difficulty, other members of the buying center become involved, thus making this dyadic relationship more complex.

Dyadic Buyer-Seller Interaction

Evans first proposed that to understand the selling process, "it is necessary to look at both parties to the sale as a dyad, not individually" [47]. Both Lombard [88] and Whyte [153] (in his study of waitresses) recognized the importance of the interaction between the participants of the dyad. Nevertheless, it was Evans who did a correlational study of the dyadic relationship between life insurance agents and their clients. He found some evidence to support the hypothesis that "the more alike the salesman and his prospect are, the greater the likelihood for a sale" [47]. A careful analysis of his reported data suggests that perceived similarity is more important than actual similarity and that similarity dimensions salient to the dyadic partners are more important than similarity in non-salient dimensions.

Tosi [139] examined the relationship between expectations, role consensus and the performance of salesmen. Role consensus, defined as the extent of agreement between parties regarding behavior pertinent to a given situation, was not a significant factor in salesman success. (Success was defined by the number of suppliers and volume obtained.) Tosi did find that a salesman perceived to be meeting his dyadic partner's expectations was likely to have less competition from other salesmen. This reduction of competition did not necessarily increase the salesman's share of the customer's business.

Brock [12], in a field experiment located in the paint department of a large retail store, explored the effect of a communicator (salesperson) being perceived as inexperienced but similar in experiences to the buyer, versus the communicator being perceived as dissimilar but experienced. Although Brock's similarity hypothesis was supported, Woodside and Davenport [167] suggest that Brock's results were *confounded* by the lack of similar-experienced and dissimilar-unexperienced treatments. They expanded Brock's design and, in the first of two studies [168], found that in the purchase of a tape-player cleaner, both perceived similarity (expression of prior purchase of the same musical tapes as the customer) and perceived expertise (based on oral instructions on how to operate the tape cleaner) increased sales. The perceived expertise condition was the most effective.

In the second experiment, a third variable, price, was introduced for the two levels of expertise. The high expertise treatment resulted in higher sales at all price levels than the low expertise treatment. A follow-up study [169] supported the strong influence of the expertise condition.

Another approach to studying dyadic interaction was taken by Willett and Pennington [154] who recorded sales conversations between fourteen appliance salesmen and their customers. They used a Bales Interaction Process Analysis to categorize the data. They found questioning and suggesting behavior on the part of the salesman lead to a high chance of success. A salesman task orientation also contributed to sales success. Viewing the dyadic relationship as a bargaining situation, Pennington [106] successfully predicted 80 percent of *purchase results.* Olshavsky [103] used a product-attribute framework to analyze the data. He found the focus on product attributes shifted during the three stages of the sales interview.

Wilson, Mathews and Monoky [159] expanded this original study of the effect of similarity upon buyer-seller interaction by incorporating the Fishbein behavioral intention paradigm as a means of measuring the influence of attributes and relevant referents on behavior. They suggest in the abstract, sales situations can be viewed as a mixed-motive game. Each member of a buyer-seller dyad strives to maximize his profit in the sales transaction, but each also recognizes a need to cooperate so that the transaction can be completed.

Strong evidence of this phenomenon was found in an experimental situation. They operationalized the treatment by collecting a demographic-personal history questionnaire and then later told the subjects that they had been matched by a "date-mate" type of computer program. The experimenters randomly assigned the subjects to the two treatment groups and a control group. A prisoner's dilemma game was used to measure behavior. Dyads who were told that they were similar cooperated more than dissimilar dyads. Although attitude towards the act of cooperation played a strong role in predicting behavior, the referent influence operated only in the cooperative condition.

These studies suggest that a member of a dyad is influenced to some extent by an assessment of the partner's expectations. Busch and Wilson [25] explored referent and expected power bases and their impact on the customer's trust in the salesman, attitude towards the salesmen, and their behavioral intentions towards action. Expert power was achieved by presenting the salesman as considerably above average on the dimensions of expertise. Referent power was operationalized by making the salesman's responses similar to the subject's responses on 84.6 percent of a series of attitude items. Buyer-seller interaction was simulated using a videotaped sales presentation. It was found that expertise is generally more effective than referent power in producing desired customer changes. Capon [31] also found support for the similarity hypothesis.

This whole area of literature is surveyed and summarized by Capon, Holbrook and Hulbert [32]. They expand and update the

Silk and Davis [124] article which reviewed the literature and offered managerial interpretations.

Dyadic Interaction as an Exchange Process

Selling may be viewed as a process in which two individuals exchange items of value. In the most simple situation, the buyer receives a product and the seller receives money. In reality, it is likely that buyer and seller exchange attributes with both physical and psychological values.

This exchange concept will be expanded later, but first it is necessary to put it in a context. Exchange does not take place in a vacuum but as part of a buyer-seller interaction process. A number of models of the sales process present a salesman-oriented model based upon the concepts of readiness, empathy and source credibility. Thompson and Evans [138] define readiness as, "an educational psychology concept that focuses attention on the individual's ability and desire to interact or communicate with another individual." Empathy is defined as "an intellectual or imaginative understanding of another's situation or as taking the role of another." Source credibility is "the trust, confidence, and faith that the respondent has in the salesman's words and actions" [138]. Salesman studied by Thompson conceived a model as shown in Fig. 2.

O'Shaughnessy [104] derives an interpersonal influence model from Kelman's [73] model of the process of opinion change and Etzioni's [46] model of power and compliance. Four sources of influence are postulated: force, patronage, attractiveness, and credibility. In applying the model, O'Shaughnessy only considers attractiveness and credibility. Given the Busch and Wilson [25] findings, the model might be reconceptualized to replace credibility with expertise and its influence upon a salesperson's credibility.

Olshavsky [102] has proposed that "to explain the behavior of a salesman-prospect dyad, it is posited that it is first necessary to know the decision dyad with respect to the task at hand" [102]. He suggests that the Newell Simon [98] information processing theory of human cognition meets the need for micro analysis of individual decision processing.

FIGURE 2

Stages in Making a Sale

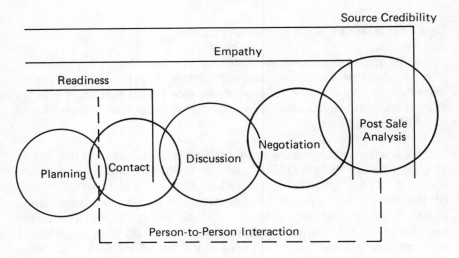

Olshavsky's approach is similar to the organizational decision process model proposed in the first part of this report. Sheth [122] developed a conceptual framework which postulates that the success of a buyer-seller interaction is:

> "a function of two distinct dimensions of interaction. The first dimension is the *content of communication* representing the substantive aspects of the purpose for which the two parties have got together. It entails suggesting, offering, promoting or negotiating a set of product-specific utilities and their expectation. . . .
>
> A second dimension of buyer-seller interaction is the style of communication. It represents the format, ritual or mannerism which the buyer and seller adopt in their interaction" [122].

Seth's model also has strong similarities to the decision process model proposed earlier. He conceives of product-specific utilities which are conceptually similar to the specification a bundle of attri-

40

butes represents to the purchase problem. The task environment, organizational influences and constraints are present in both models.

Wilson [156] proposed a dyadic process model that is similar to many of the above models. His model is basically concerned with the development of a long-term buyer-seller relationship rather than "one-shot" selling situations. It begins with an initial meeting between the buyer and seller and moves through a number of stages which presumably take place over time and a number of meetings. This does not preclude the adaption of the model to single contact situations.

Fig. 3 depicts the model. A similarity exists to the Lavidge-Steiner [78] and AIDA [130] models as well as the other models described above. The duration of the stages overlap each other as a number of activities may be carried on simultaneously. The requirements of the basic stages must be met in order to move to the advanced stages of the model. The different stages are meant only to suggest that they are the focus of the major efforts of the dyad and the other stages receive less effort during the current stage. It could be hypothesized that if one could trace interaction over time, the focus of the interaction would change as shown in the model. The model proposed here attempts to reflect the influence of some of the sales research conducted in recent years.

There are two basic assumptions underlying the model:

1. The buyer is attempting to secure a bundle of attributes, both tangible and psychological, from the seller. These attributes may be related to the product, to the company and to the salesman. To illustrate, the product may provide performance attributes that are highly valued by the buyer, the company may provide general reputation attributes, and the salesman may provide personal service and reliability attributes. The concept broadens Sheth's product-specific utilities.
2. The buyer-seller relationship develops over a period of time. Examples of this type of relationship are numerous in organizational buying situations, personal estate planning, life insurance situations, and in some retail situations where strong customer loyalties are developed.

41

FIGURE 3

A Dyadic Sales Process Model

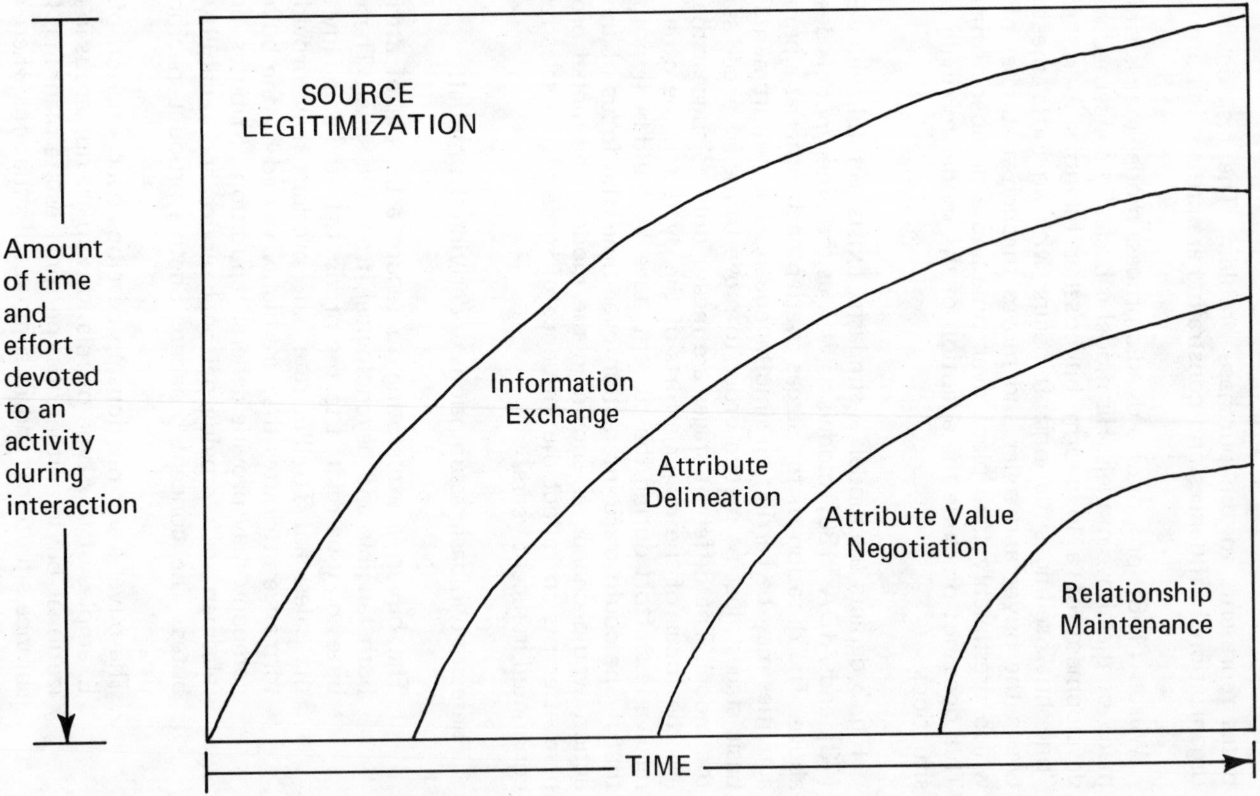

SOURCE LEGITIMIZATION

Information Exchange

Attribute Delineation

Attribute Value Negotiation

Relationship Maintenance

TIME

Amount of time and effort devoted to an activity during interaction

Source Legitimization

The model assumes the buyer and seller come together in something akin to the Howard and Sheth [14] extensive problem-solving situation. Monoky, Mathews and Wilson [92] found that sources of information are differentially preferred as a function of the type of selling situation. The situations in their study ranged from new task to rebuy situations. These data suggest that the salesman's role shifts over time as the buying situation moves from the new task to the rebuy situation.

In the new task situation, the salesperson needs to develop source credibility and legitimization. Unless this basic acceptability is developed, further communication is likely to become quite ineffective if not impossible. Based on the studies discussed earlier [167, 168, 25], it seems likely that in this early stage of the sales process the salesperson attribute of "expert" may dominate the attribute of "similarity."

The basic objective of this first stage is to establish the salesman as a legitimate and credible partner in the dyadic interaction process. It is likely that this process continues through the early interactions of the dyad.

Information Exchange—Problem Identification

This stage involves bounding the problem to be solved through a purchase. The amount and nature of the information exchange is likely to be a function of the relationship established in the previous stage. A salesperson perceived as an expert is likely to be given more information quicker than other salespersons. All salespersons may get the standard type of information but the more favored salesperson may get additional data such as which attributes are important and who is the key decision maker in the buying center.

The salesperson attempts to establish the nature of the problem in order to be able to suggest an attribute package that will result in a sale. The salesperson is also concerned about positioning the attribute package with respect to competition and in developing a strong bargaining base.

Attribute Delineation

In this stage, the dyad develops the bundle of attributes that will be exchanged. Many of the attributes will be explicitly discussed—for example, product features and credit terms—while other attributes may be implicitly determined. Olshavsky [102] observed that the salesman clearly influenced attribute determination and evaluation. Again, this study is limited by its one-shot nature in a retail setting where the buyer may lack the buying expertise that is present in organizational purchasing. Nevertheless, the study does indicate that although parties developed the attribute set, the salesman can have a major influence in the development of the attribute set through guidance and direction of the buyer.

It seems reasonable to expect the determinant attributes to shift over time. Attributes such as product quality, delivery, etc., may remain important but not determinant in how the dyad relationship is maintained. Interpersonal exchanges between the buyer and the seller may become more important as the purchasing problem moves to the rebuy situation. Similarity between the members of the dyad may become a more powerful influence at this stage.

Also of importance is the nature of the product. If there are clear product differences they may be used to differentiate the various attribute packages. However, if substantial product differences do not exist, then intangible attributes may dominate.

Attribute Value Negotiation

The determining of the attribute set and the exchange rate of each attribute can be viewed as a bargaining process. Pennington [106] concluded "that bargaining behavior between customers and salespersons, although not overwhelming in frequency or volumes, exerts an important impact on ultimate purchase outcomes." He found that the greatest bargaining was "on the presentation of concession limits—such as presentation of prices, delivery dates, product features—by the salesman, and statements of desired price ranges, styles, and product features by the customers." These findings support the notion of bargaining the rate of exchange on attributes. The value of individual attributes may be subject to limited negotiation. The

44

seller will be likely to attempt to increase the importance in the choice of his strong attributes while the buyer may attempt to suggest an increased importance of the seller's weaker attributes in hopes of gaining an increased level of other attributes. For example, the buyer may suggest that price is important when he really hopes to gain better credit terms. In other words, there may be a trading of the amount of each attribute that will make up the final package of attributes.

Relationship Maintenance

In the final stage of the model, the dyad maintains and builds upon its relationship. New personal attributes of the relationship may develop which enable it to grow from a business relationship to a more personal business/friendship relationship. A certain amount of implicit bargaining over exchange values may take place, particularly if problems with performance attributes arise. From a salesperson's point of view, the maintenance of friendly accounts is much easier than the development of new accounts.

Dyadic Interaction: An Exchange Process

The relationship of dyadic partners can be measured through the attribute sets that link them together. Sheth [122] suggests that the dyadic relationship can be expressed by performing a dimensional analysis of the vectors of buyer-seller expectations. The distance between the buyer and seller in space represents the degree of incompatibility of the dyad.

Another approach is to view the dyadic relationships as an exchange process. The basic premise of the concept of an exchange process derives from Homan's [63:7] contention that "elementary social behavior is the face-to-face contact between individuals, in which the reward each gets from the behavior of the other is relatively direct and immediate." He suggests that this interaction can yield a profit to both parties if you "give the other man behavior that is more valuable to him than it is costly to you and to get from him behavior that is more valuable to you than it is costly to him" (p. 62).

45

Homan's concept may be extrapolated to the buyer-seller dyad as the notion that each individual develops a bundle of attributes that can be exchanged and which have *utility* to him. The successful dyad exchanges these bundles of attributes at a profit. On one level, the salesman provides product and receives payment while on another level he may provide advice and receive esteem. The buyer receives product and gives payment. He also may receive advice which helps him solve a purchasing problem and give esteem as payment. The advice may not directly relate to the salesman's product.

Again, to simplify the discussion, the linkage of the value of the attribute to the buyer or seller may depend upon the ability of the attribute to satisfy the needs of others within either the buyer's or seller's firms. This linkage is recognized but because of the limited focus of this paper, it will be ignored. The exploration of these linkages needs a paper itself.

To illustrate the exchange concept, assume a purchasing situation in which the buyer must choose between the offerings of three salespersons. Each salesperson goes through the early stages of the process model of Fig. 3, i.e., source legitimization, information exchange, and attribute delineation. The individual salesperson attempts to establish a set of attributes that have value to the buyer and, if possible, are different from his competitor's offerings. Hence, the buyer is confronted with three unique sets of attributes (X_{nqj}). The subscript j refers to the salesman, the subscript n refers to the attributes, and the subscript q refers to the level of attributes in the set.

The buyer must select X_{nq1}, X_{nq2}, or X_{nq3}. It is assumed that each of these attributes has some cost to the buyer and that the buyer seeks to maximize his profit in the transaction, that is, the buyer seeks the maximum multi-attribute utility (MAU). The choice is now to select from the utility set that U_{nqj} with the highest value. It is assumed that individual attributes can be positive or negative and that the summing of the attribute utility nets out to the "profit" of the relationship.

Profit in this situation is a nebulous concept but may be thought of as the netting out of positive attributes and negative attributes. For example, price could be a negative attribute. It is suggested that exploratory research may eliminate the need for the profit notion

46

and that a summation of the values of positive and negative attributes will be sufficient.

Recalling that the attribute sets contain product, company and salesman attributes, it is then possible to examine the impact of the salesman upon the total value of the attribute package.

The exchange notion which enters in is that the salesman must allocate his time and effort over a number of buyers and he presumably seeks to maximize his total return by choosing to deal with those buyers who offer him a "profit." Therefore, the buyer must present a set of attributes to the salesman, the principal one being the monetary value of the order. This concept may become even more relevant in this era of shortages and sellers' markets.

Measurement of the Value Attribute Sets

There has been a considerable amount of research conducted on MAU models, both in the laboratory and in the field. Huber [67, 68] presents a useful summary of the state of the art. The attribute set in the selling dyad is likely to be much more complex than those that have been reported in the literature.

A general additive form of the multi-attribute utility model is

$$U(x) = \sum_{n-1}^{n} b_n U(X_{nqj})$$

where b_n is a measure of the relative importance of the attributes and can be represented on a 0 to 1.0 scale. $U(X_{nq})$ is the utility value of attribute X_n at the q level. It is suggested that since the attribute sets include salesman attributes which are unique to the individual, it might be useful at this early stage of development to describe the utility sets as $U(X_{njq})$ where j refers to the salesmen. If in fact the attribute sets prove to be consistent across salesmen, then only the level of an attribute need be used. If uncertainty associated with the attributes is considered, a subjective expected multi-attribute model (SEMAU) is created. Wilson and Busch [158], in a test of the association between an attitude intention model and an SEU model,

47

found a high correlation between the predictions of the two models. Although the models are theoretically different, their robustness may allow them to approximate the same results.

Huber [69] had similar results when he attempted to use different models to predict individual preferences on stimuli defined by physical characteristics. He suggests that the robustness of his models allows him to approximate preference surfaces in spite of theoretical invalidity. The large literature on expectation models may provide some guidance in developing empirical tests of the MAU proposition.

NESTING THE MODELS

The decision process model depicted in Fig. 1 specifies the structural elements of the buyer's side of the dyad. A similar structural model could be postulated for the salesperson with the linkages between the individuals closely tied to the attribute sets. The addition of the dyadic sales process makes the structural model dynamic in the sense that the elements change over time as a function of the stage of the dyadic interaction.

In designing research, the structural decision process model suggests that we might study the interaction process from an information/decision processing framework. The inclusion of the organizational and task environments and buying center influences suggests factors that mediate information/decision processing.

The sales process model suggests the need to consider the stage of the dyad relationship in developing an information decision processing framework. Changes in the attribute set likely occur over time and need to be incorporated into a decision process model.

The two models capture a number of the key factors that researchers and theorists suggest as fundamental to the study of dyadic interaction in organizations. Careful research is now required to test and clarify the concepts of the models.

THE DYADIC PARADIGM WITH SPECIFIC APPLICATION TOWARD INDUSTRIAL MARKETING

Thomas V. Bonoma
Graduate School of Business
University of Pittsburgh

Richard Bagozzi
Graduate School of Management
University of California at Berkeley

Gerald Zaltman
Graduate School of Business
University of Pittsburgh

There is ample evidence in the literature of a widespread "crisis of consciousness" in marketing. Everywhere one looks old preconceptions are being challenged, previously agreed-upon concepts are being threatened, and general dissatisfaction is being voiced. The purpose of this report is to suggest that there is at least one identifiable cause for the crisis of consciousness in marketing, and that recognizing it can lead to a partial remedy.

Marketing science appears to have reached a threshold of progress, a threshold which every scientific endeavor from physics to psychology has had to confront and pass. There is a lesson to be learned about marketing behavior by observing what it was that was needed in other areas for those areas to pass beyond this threshold.

Basically the lesson is this: Scientific analysis of marketing behavior must be structurally, as well as functionally, posed in a fashion similar to that in which the target behaviors occur. The phenomena of marketing must be considered in terms of the way in which the phenomena actually occur. It is suggested that explicit recognition of this dictum can enable marketing to resolve its crisis of consciousness, to pass the current threshold, and to permit increasingly more meaningful analysis of marketing behavior.

This report will examine a new marketing perspective, called the "dyadic paradigm," and will distinguish it from traditional ways of construing marketing. Although the field of industrial marketing is the field under study, the reader should bear in mind that the commentary on the dyadic perspective is intended equally for all marketing relations.

Next, a conceptual framework is presented for viewing marketing dyads. Finally, the principle of the dyadic paradigm is presented with an example of the purchasing agent-industrial salesman interaction.

THE UNIT PARADIGM AND THE DYADIC PARADIGM

Whether the focus is industrial marketing or consumer behavior, the current overwhelmingly dominant analytic tendency in marketing is to attempt to regard those variables modifying behavior as *single* factors, such as an organization, a salesman, a buyer, etc. Thus, in industrial marketing, the dominant treatment focuses either on patterns of decision making within a single organization or, macroscopically, on a single organization as it is affected by environmental factors. Sheth [122], for example, poses a model of industrial buying which characterizes this activity as it is affected by certain forces, such as intraorganizational expectations, life styles, and organization size.

Kotler and others [76, 77] have characterized the general marketing unit as surrounded by an "external environment," one which imposes "constraints" on the activities of that unit. Again, Champion [34] classifies organizational models into "machine models," goal models and decision models, all of which assume that the marketing organization is best represented as a closed system of stimuli which directly and totally determine unit output.

Those readers familiar with the general strategy of reductionism [64, 18] will recognize that the basic paradigm under consideration by current marketing analysts is one in which the analytical problems associated with marketing behavior are initially blasted into small parts (the consumer, the manager, the rack jobber, the distribution channel), following which a causal analysis of the behavior of each of the parts is attempted. Thus the behavior of *single* buyers or organizations is considered a direct and usually linear function of the imposition of certain stimuli from the environment.

We term this perspective in marketing, in which an "organism" (e.g. industrial buyer, consumer) is presented with a stimulus from without (e.g., advertisement) and the effect of this stimulus on his behavior the "unit paradigm." It couples reductionism (the basic units of marketing) with a stimulus-response view of behavior. It is assumed that by studying the components of marketing behavior, and by making sense of what makes these basic parts tick, the little explanatory pieces may eventually be put together as a rough, but accurate, composite of all marketing behaviors making up the marketing system [51].

It is only natural that marketers focus on the behavior of one organization, one channel,[1] or one industrial purchasing department at a time [122] for, after all, isn't it true that if these elusive variables and properties can be identified in one study unit, we can then generalize our new-found knowledge to cover all similar firms?

Such is the powerful logic and motivation of the "unit paradigm"; it is also often its false promise. The unit paradigm has been the initial perspective of every physical, biological, and social science yet devised, and it has likewise had to be abandoned, at least partially, by every discipline which eventually provided meaningful commentary on man or nature [149, 152].

Perhaps two simple examples will make our premise more vivid. Psychologists have long sought answers to the problems of social perception [9]. Throughout the nineteenth century it was common to view the perceiver, through the lens of the unit paradigm, as an isolated actor exposed to varying "stimuli" and making what sense

---

[1]See the criticism of traditional distribution channel models [126, 127].

of these he could by combining the components of each stimulus according to several basic and irreducible laws of perceptual learning.

Perceptual "errors" were thus possible, and were "committed" by every perceiver who "saw" the enticing "moving" arrows, "dancing" women, and other illusory scenes of movement actually consisting of perfectly stationary lights. It was not until Max Wertheimer [61] became fascinated with a child's toy stroboscope and turned his skills to explaining these "errors of perception," that psychologists began to understand that they were not necessarily errors at all.

Perception, Wertheimer tells us, cannot be reduced into its "component" parts, for there often are no "components" in the sense of unitary stimuli. Rather, flashing lights must be interpreted in their context, with regard to the position of other flashing lights. When this is done, when the stimulus is interpreted in the context of its field, *and only then,* do matters such as apparent movements and other perceptual illusions become understandable. There are patterns in perception and to violate these patterns with our analytic devices is to insure that we cannot understand the phenomena we wish to explain.

Again, and moving closer to the area of marketing, social psychologists have long been concerned with the variance between an individual's attitude and his behavior. According to the most recent surveys, the correlation between attitudes and action almost exactly approximates 0.00 [40]. How can this be? We intuitively *know* that what people say and what they do are not *totally* unrelated. Consumer behavior and social psychology have extremely complex reductionistic stimulus-response views of both attitudes and acts. Hence, we ought to be able to predict the concordance of attitudes and acts for each individual or at least for groups of individuals.

The fallacy here is the same as that with perception: human *social* behavior occurs *in the contexts* of (a) other individuals, and (b) disparate social situations. We "manage" our attitudes in order to present the most flattering, most favorable and most consistent image of ourselves to others [132]; as long as the audiences in different social situations differ, we are free to present two quite different pictures of ourselves and we do so in order to maximize our *interactive* rewards from the two situations.

Again, social situations differ in their type and implication for the participant, to ask an individual what his attitude is toward black salesmen, or General Motors or Thrill detergent, for example, is to completely miss the point that behavior is situation-specific. Do we mean how would the consumer behave toward a black salesman in front of other customers in a store, or in the privacy of his home, or on his doorstep? Disregard for the context has rendered traditional attitude theory and attitude measurement in marketing, as in social psychology, a generally frustrating endeavor [86, 132].

The Dyadic Paradigm

How are these lessons to be incorporated into a perspective for marketing which recognizes the basically social character of that activity? We propose the adoption of a new perspective in marketing, one which can be called the "dyadic paradigm." It contains, as its first two parts, a restatement of what we have learned about behavior from other disciplines, and, as its third part, a recommendation for the marketing focus. It is this: (1) behavior, of whatever kind, cannot be analyzed or explained independently of the context in which it occurs; (2) to "reduce" explanations into constructs (however simple) which violate the structure of the interaction under consideration, is to guarantee confusion, and, most importantly, (3) since marketing is a *social* activity, marketers should adopt a social perspective for marketing analyses. This perspective assumes that the basic unit of social activity is the dyad. Dyadic (two-person, two-organization, buyer-seller) units are the smallest irreducible units of social analysis. The first two columns of Table I summarize the discussion to this point.

In order to better understand the differences between a unit versus a dyadic perspective on marketing, consider the case of the industrial buyer-seller relationship. As shown in Table I, the usual approach in industrial marketing has been to regard the situation as a unit; a single buyer (or buying department) within an organization is examined as a respondent to certain external stimuli which affects the activities. Thus, one can study the "efficiency" or "risk potential" of the buying process under different communication strategies [82].

But this typical construal seriously violates the sense of what ordinarily transpires in industrial marketing. Actually, the industrial

53

TABLE 1
Three Fundamental Paradigms in Marketing

FEATURE	PERSPECTIVE		
	UNIT PARADIGM	DYADIC PARADIGM	SYSTEM PARADIGM
Structure	*Learning Model* $S \to O \to R$	*Social Model* $A \leftrightarrow B$	*Embeddation Model* $\boxed{\begin{array}{c} C \\ A \leftrightarrow B \end{array}}$
Major Process	Exogenous Influence	Reciprocal Influence	System maintenance, integration, goal attainment, etc.
Explanatory Mechanisms	Stimulus-Response	Interdependence	Functional Requisites
Typical Models or Pre-Models	Sheth's Organizational Buying Model Attitude and Multi-Attribute Models Information Processing Models	Ammer's "Realistic Reciprocity" Cadotte and Stern's Interorganizational Relations Model Bagozzi's Exchange Model Weigand's Purchasing Notions	Lazar's Marketing Systems Kotler's Publics
Typical Foci	Rationality Efficiency Closed Systems Predictability Control Input-Output	Social Interdependence Exchange Power and Influence Relations Bargaining and Negotiation Mutual Problem Solving Explanation and Understanding	Open Systems Organic Analogy Part-Whole Relations Descriptive Charts Homeostasis and Equilibrium
Typical Problems	Reductionistic Mechanistic Violates *social* character of marketing Static focus Neglect of the meaning of products, actions, etc.	Marketing Relations more closely resemble systems	Descriptive in present stage of development System processes often are undeterminable Currently untestable

buyer is embedded in a series of relationships both intraorganization-ally and interorganizationally. He has certain dyadic relations with colleagues in both vertical and horizontal organizational structures affecting the pending decision. Also, the supplier-buyer *relationships* obtaining in the real world are major ones for understanding buying decisions. None of these can be suitably viewed as external stimuli impinging on an "independent" actor's decision-making processes. Rather, they are dyadic relations, the context of which makes the buyer's decisions predictable.

Generally speaking, then, it is best to describe the industrial mar-keter as embedded in an *interdependent nexus* of social relationships, a nexus which both modifies and makes sense of his behaviors. Though space does not permit, a similar argument can be made re-garding consumer behavior. In fact, the recent rise of "consumerism" [120] can be viewed as a consequence of the unit assumption: Marketers, advertisers and sales staff have consistently treated con-sumer relationships as stimulus-response systems, entities to be *acted upon* rather than entities with whom one interacts.

Selected Implications of a Dyadic Perspective

A central question must now be addressed: Does changing the focus of marketing from a unit to a dyadic viewpoint really change anything, beyond the words? To illuminate the dyadic viewpoint, some general hypotheses drawn from industrial marketing are pre-sented, first in the unit context, then with the hypothesis restated as it would occur if placed in a dyadic perspective.

    1a. *Unit Perspective:* "The greater the perceived risk in a spe-cific buying decision, the more likely it is that the purchase will be decided jointly. . . " [122].

    1b. *Dyadic Perspective:* Judgments of risk, like all other in-terpersonal variables, are determined in negotiations with others. The interactive variables determining risk judgments include intraorganizational discussions and interorganiza-tional (suppliers) presentations. When such negotiated judg-ments reach a consensus of risky decision parameters, buying decisions will tend to *overtly* include more individ-uals in the firm, *if* dyadic relationships permit.

2a. *Unit Perspective:* ". . . at least some of the industrial buying decisions are determined by *ad hoc* situational factors. . ." [122].

2b. *Dyadic Perspective: All* industrial buying decisions are affected by (a) the pattern of social relations within the focal firm, (b) the interrelationships with other firms, and (c) "situational" factors. *No* buying decision is independently determined by any of these.

3a. *Unit Perspective:* "Both bargaining and politicking are nonrational and inefficient methods of conflict resolution; the buying organization suffers from these conflicts." [122].

3b. *Dyadic Perspective:* Bargaining, conflict, and, hence, conflict resolution are the essence of purchasing organizations and purchasing decisions; they can be rational or irrational, but they are inevitably present in any system which negotiates, exchanges, and bargains for influence.

The above contrasts should make the unit vs. dyadic paradigms more clear. In the first case, a single actor is defined as responding to stimuli, hence "bargaining," "negotiating," and "politicking" are inappropriate and "nonrational." In the second case, pairs of actors are seen as the basic unit of analysis and negotiation is engaged in regarding everything, from the nature of reality to the nature of the impending decision. In the first case, risk is a unitary concept which can be perceived by purchasers and is said to affect their behavior. In the second, risk is determined jointly by intraorganizational groups, as well as being affected by interorganizational relationships.

Current Work on the Dyadic Paradigm

There is some interesting and encouraging preliminary work being done on dyadic perspective. Cohen has urged an interpersonal approach for the study of consumer decision making and he reports data showing the utility of this approach [36]. Ammer [7] has noted the strong tendency in buyer-seller relations toward "realistic reciprocity," that is, for dyads of buyers and sellers to establish transactional relations over time. He cautions us against focusing on just industrial buyer behavior, for example, without taking these dyadic relations into account. Levy and Zaltman [85] present a persuasive reconceptualization of marketing relationships generally which explicitly focuses on exchange processes and hence, on two-person relationships as the basic unit of analysis. A similar line of inquiry, somewhat more formalized, has been pursued by Bagozzi [10].

And finally, Cardotte and Stern [27] present a most interesting model of interorganizational relationships which includes, as a specific theoretical predictor, the degree and type of interdependencies between organizational components. Their radical model, for example, predicts *no* organizational interaction where there is no interorganizational interdependency. Table I lists these and other examples of a fledgling dyadic perspective in marketing analyses.

Why Not a Systems Perspective?

Finally there is the question of why we do not advocate a systems perspective for marketing analyses, as is becoming prominent in the literature [80]. It can be argued that a dyadic model is a fledgling systems perspective and, therefore, that the former is only a special case of the latter. Though there is some validity to this observation, we believe there are compelling reasons at this "state of the art" for *not* moving toward a full-fledged systems perspective.

In summary, they are these:

1. At this stage of its development, systems "theory" is primarily a descriptive tool (e.g., the flow chart) which does not admit of rigorous hypothesis formulation, testing, or theory-formation. In fact, and in spite of the claims of its proponents [15], systems theory at this time must be regarded as an extremely promising *future* way of looking at marketing behavior. Its current utility is limited by its rudimentary development.
2. While systems theory may in fact present a more accurate view of the marketing world than a dyadic perspective, rigorous theories and confirmed empirical relationships from social psychology and sociology employing a dyadic perspective are more readily available for extension to the marketing discipline. It is important to remember that we are not advocating a dyadic model simply because theories and findings exist. When it is considered that the dyadic model *is* a de-

57

graded full systems perspective and that readily tested versions of it exist in various forms, it may well be the optimal tool for the present.

3. A systems perspective ordinarily commits its advocate to certain generic assumptions about both system performance and/or subsystem process. In the biological disciplines, for example, it is clear that cell processes are mirrored in organ processes; in organizational theory, it is extremely doubtful that individual behavior is replicated by organizational "actions."

All of these points are summarized in Table I. It seems very premature to commit ourselves to such strictures when there exists an alternative perspective which does not require such commitments, yet which does not commit the levels-of-analysis errors entailed in the unit assumption.

The true test of any perspective shift in a discipline, however, is whether it permits greater clarity. We turn now to a preliminary general theoretical statement.

Notes Toward A Theory

In order to illustrate a dyadic paradigm's utility as a base for generating and testing marketing theory, a framework is presented for viewing behavior in the marketing dyad. The concepts presented are intended as the foundation for a general theory of marketing interaction. The articulation of the concepts—in cause and effect relations, social processes, etc.—form the major explanatory mechanisms for interpreting exchanges, transactions, and conflicts in marketing relations.

Two cautionary statements are necessary. First, the dyadic sense of marketing has been included in this general model as represented by only one specific class of variables. Other variables (e.g., individualistic, normative) are included which are not intended as relational in this presentation but rather which form a "fixed context" or "frame" [52] within which relational marketing interactions occur.

58

The second point is closely tied to the first: A "radical" dyadic perspective on marketing could contend that *all* the other variable classes included in this general construal are also relational. That is, it is quite possible to argue [117] that person-specific variables, social structures, and normative variables (also included in the model presented below) are also negotiated, social, and hence systematic, if not dyadic, in nature. It can be readily contended that the way an individual sees a detergent, for example, is through a negotiated settlement between the actor's past social history (e.g., his parents and peers), the manufacturer's packaging strategy, the retailer's display, etc. Thus, the "other classes" of variables besides the relational can be thought of more properly as *different kinds* of relational variables. The treatment here of personal and/or normative variables as fixed is only to highlight the dependence of other variables on the relationship between the marketer and his clients.

The reader might be reminded that all variables may be social at various points in the exposition. There is no facet of human individual, dyadic or group life that cannot be ultimately traced to a social origin [131].

Relational Variables. The structure of any dyad may be represented as an interrelationship among four classes of variables (see Table 2). The primary scientific phenomena to be explained in the dyad are relational variables. Relational variables are concepts specifying the nature of the connections binding actors in a dyad. They are characteristics of the interaction rather than attributes of the actors or properties of outside forces. Typical relational variables include dependence, power, influence, conflict, reciprocity, exchange, intensity, and competition [90].

In general, the basic research questions in regard to relational variables are (1) Why do (or do not) certain relations come about and persist (e.g., the exchange relation between a wholesaler and retailer)? (2) Why do relations change or disintegrate? and (3) What are the causes and consequences of marketing relations? The thesis of this section is that the study of the various forms of dyadic relations, the conditions producing and influencing them, and their implications are the distinctive task of the marketing discipline.

Social Structural Variables. Social structural variables comprise another class of concepts crucial for understanding marketing rela-

TABLE 2
The Structure of the Marketing Dyad

Variable Class	Location or Source of Variable	Theoretical Example
Relational Variables	Interation	Dependence Power Conflict Exchange Reciprocity Intensity
Social Structural Variables	Situation	Third party interdependence Horizontal and Vertical differentiation
Social Actor Variables	Actors	Comparison levels History of reward Personality Characteristics; within actor structure Capabilities and resources of actors
Normative Variables	Interaction, Situation, and Actors	Social norms, roles and standards Goals Role Expectations

tions. They may be defined as (1) the conditions of the situation within which the dyadic relation occurs and (2) the social positions that the actors in the dyad occupy. The conditions of any situation refer to the pattern of opportunities and constraints which shape the behaviors and expectations of the actors in a dyad. For example, the nature of the interaction between an industrial salesman and a purchasing agent will be influenced by the social structure within the purchasing department and the relations between the purchasing department and other social actors. The formalization, standardization, centralization and complexity of activities in the purchasing department will determine the communication patterns and the outcome of the salesman-purchasing agent interchange [172].

A second aspect of structural variables arises from the social positions that the actors in the dyad occupy. In general, social actors will differ in the groups to which they belong, their status within these groups, and the claims and perogatives accorded them. Membership in various groups affects role relations and social interaction through two distinct processes.

First, horizontal differentiation arises by virtue of membership in diverse groups [172]. Of course, one cannot belong to a group unless there are at least two groups defined in relation to one another. Thus, processes of affiliation, conformity, attraction and so forth, arise from one's identification with a particular sex, religion, race, club, occupation, or ethnic group. Consumer behavior researchers have long recognized the influence that reference groups have on consumer purchases [44].

Second, vertical or hierarchical differentiation occurs when social actors occupy positions of differing status [19]. Typically, each actor in a dyadic relation will possess differing rights and obligations in numerous groups, and these factors can shape the nature of the interaction. For instance, a purchasing agent may be limited in the discretion and degree of commitment he may make to a salesman by virtue of the power and expertise that the engineering department has in intraorganizational relations. Hierarchical differentiation such as this is evident in disparities in prestige, power, credibility, income, age, education, and other parameters common to social structures. Research questions associated with social structural variables include (1) How do "situational" factors and aspects of social differentiation influence the emergence, course, or decline of a dyadic relation? and (2) What are the consequences that dyadic relations have for the social structure?

61

Social Actor Variables. A third class of concepts which may aid in the interpretation of dyadic interactions are social actor variables. Social actor variables refer to the characteristics of individuals that contribute to or hinder the resolution of dyadic relations. Typical social actor variables include one's history of rewards, the standard by which one evaluates the relative satisfaction of outcomes (comparison level) [136], the lowest level of outcomes that one could currently obtain from some available alternative social relationship (comparison level for alternatives) [136], personality variables (self esteem, internal control of reinforcements, motivation), physical resources, personal capabilities (cognitive complexity, analytical ability), and expectational concepts such as purposes and intentions. Marketing research guided by the unit paradigm assumes that whenever the same stimulus object appears—other things being equal—people will respond in the same predictable way.

The marketer need only search for those stimuli (package, colors, credible sources, information) which elicit the desired response (purchase). The fact that people do respond differently, or not at all, to the same stimulus leads the follower of the unit paradigm on a search for other "situational" or "exogenous" stimuli which confound or wash out the predicted S-R hypothesis. In contrast, the dyadic paradigm views consumer and organizational behavior, and even perceptions, as a negotiated social process whereby people interact, explore their thoughts and feelings, exchange information, and perhaps evolve to new or novel positions and relationships.

The reason a buyer may find a product or service undesirable may lie not in the espoused or internal attitude toward the object, but rather in the interpersonal meanings the object has for the "individual" as he enjoys or suffers the social relationships making up his life. This includes his relationship with the marketer.

The research questions of interest in regard to social actor variables are (1) How do the characteristics of social actors constrain or liberate aspects of dyadic relations? and (2) What are the processes or stages that individuals experience as a dyad evolves?

Normative Variables. Normative variables are the final class of concepts useful for understanding marketing dyads. Normative variables are concerned with how people, or categories of people, ought to behave. They provide guidelines for action and are reflected in the expectations, plans, and behavioral self-monitoring of social actors. Moreover, fulfillment of norms often evokes positive reactions from others, while the violation of norms may summon negative reactions. Typical normative variables include rules, role expectations, and laws [60, 164].

Normative variables may be classified in one of three categories: individual, relational, and situational. "Individual norms" refer to the personal orientations of people irrespective of present interaction partners or situations. They are ideational, general in scope, static and unidirectional in that they are not contingent upon the response of others or contextual demands. Thus, for instance, salesmen are coached (by *others,* of course) to "always wear a smile," "be aggressive," or "act as if the customer is always right." Since individual norms require that one manage a particular presentation of self, they are conceptually similar to unit paradigmatic principles wherein a set of stimuli are controlled to induce a response. Relational norms, in contrast, govern the behaviors of social actors in dyads. They specify how one ought to act *vis-à-vis* another, what mutual outcomes are to be expected, and when a relationship should continue, evolve, or breakup.

Relational norms are dynamic, bi-directional and, to a certain extent, fluid and open to constant reinterpretation and modification. Interpersonal trust is perhaps the best example of a relational norm in marketing with the "marketing concept" its most visible manifestation.

Finally, situational norms suggest alternative behavior to be followed when certain circumstances arise. For example, Kotler suggests that during periods of shortage, firms should find ways to make existing scarce products go further or find substitute products or sources of energy [76]. Suggested alternative contingencies include: switching scarce raw materials and fuels into the products that have higher profitability, directing different amounts of sales effort to various size customers, and reprogramming the marketing mix.

The important questions to ask with respect to normative variables are: (1) What are the effects of rules and norms on dyadic processes? (2) When and how are norms invoked as guides for behavior? and

63

(3) What are the roles of norms in the social structure and how do they arise and change?

An Application of the Dyadic Paradigm

Let us now consider, as an illustration, a purchasing agent—salesman interaction which one of the authors had the opportunity to observe in the course of a recent consulting assignment. The example is unique in that one of the authors was subsequently able to meet alone with the purchasing agent and salesman to discuss the events. We shall analyze this particular buyer/seller event in terms of four concepts: *credibility,* which concerns the extent to which a buyer, for example, perceives a salesman as trustworthy and reliable; *status inconsistency* which, in this illustration, refers to the discrepancy between two roles a buyer or salesman may choose to enact; *empathy,* which is the ability to put one's self in another person's place; and *interpersonal attraction,* which refers to the extent to which rewards are exchanged by the interacting parties. All four concepts are basically and irreducibly relational in nature, although they are often treated as individual attributes.

This illustration involved the purchase of capital equipment by a container manufacturer. The purchasing agent and salesman had not met prior to the encounter described here. The salesman displayed strong empathetic skills, no doubt developed through countless interactions with industrial purchasing agents. The salesman was particularly skillful in empathizing with the purchasing agent's status inconsistency. The salesman made half-serious, half-joking references to the fact that senior management didn't appreciate the purchasing agent's role. In response, the purchasing agent identified a few such individuals. The salesman correctly concluded that these individuals were key influentials in the purchase decision process and he later met with each of these people. He was careful, however, to display some limited deference (another relational concept) to the purchasing agent, thus enhancing the purchasing agent's sense of importance as a gatekeeper (a particular role relationship in the buying process).

The purchasing agent repeatedly expressed this sense of importance by referring to past decisions in which he believed he was instrumental in selecting the supplier, once a purchase decision had

64

been made, a matter of great importance to the salesman if it were true (as it was in this case).

Thus, the purchasing agent was in a subordinate position with respect to selected management personnel relevant to the buying decision but in a superior position with regard to salesmen. The salesman was able to use this information to advantage but probably would not have had the information if he had been unable to relate to the agent in an empathetic way. Note in this case that neither empathy nor status inconsistency—two critical phenomena in this buyer-seller situation—can exist unless at least two persons are involved. The unit paradigm perspective would likely not have suggested these explanatory concepts.

Credibility and interpersonal attraction were also important factors in the situation described here. Credibility, as a relational concept, involved a judgment by the purchasing agent of the salesman's expertise. Note that this involves the interaction of one person's judgmental processes with another person's expertise. (Both judgment and expertise must also be defined interpersonally, although space limitations do not permit an elaboration of this.) The salesman seemed to have established credibility in two ways. One was through a display of technical knowledge cast in terms which made this quality obvious to the purchasing agent. The salesman stressed the value of his line of equipment in terms of production problems the firm was having. The salesman later indicated to one of the researchers that he had talked with someone from the purchasing company's production division two weeks prior to his visit with the purchasing agent. This involved interaction with the agent's environment. The agent was unaware of this and consequently was rather impressed with the salesman's insight into certain technical problems.

Another technique the salesman used was to mention other firms in the area with whom he dealt on a regular basis. Thus, the salesman used to advantage his relationship with other companies and with someone from the agent's own production department to influence the nature of his relationship with the purchasing agent.

There was not a great deal of interpersonal attraction for either party. For example, the salesman made an attempt at a joke. Thus entertainment was proffered in solicitation of laughter (a form of approval). The purchasing agent remained quite sober, however, which made the salesman feel decidedly awkward for several moments. This was the general tenor of the rest of the discussion. Later, in response to questions posed to each party separately, both men indicated they would not object to having the other as a neighbor but neither would they freely choose the other as a neighbor.

Here, too, credibility and, more obviously, interpersonal attraction are basically relational concepts whose meaning and importance are best elicited when viewed from a dyadic perspective. The salesman is viewed as credible only in an interpersonal setting in which the purchasing agent's own technical knowledge and the perceived technical knowledge of other salesmen, both real and idealized, are important factors.

Conclusions and Implications

This report has argued for a major shift in perspective when studying marketing behavior. This shift involves a move from the reductionist approach to one which better reflects the actual ways in which marketing phenomena are structured. The adoption of a dyadic paradigm over a unit paradigm changes the focal unit of analysis away from an individual or an organization to a relationship. Perhaps the two most important implications of this shift are that it changes the way the investigator poses questions and it changes his basic way of viewing the situation. Once one alters the way questions are posed and, consequently, the mix of concepts used to explain reactions, a long stride has been taken toward better understanding.

Our understanding of marketing under a unit paradigm probably differs radically from our understanding of marketing under a dyadic paradigm. If there is any lesson to be learned from the disciplines which have matured beyond the point now occupied by marketing research, it is that now is the time to make a change.

ORGANIZATIONAL BUYING CENTER: A RESEARCH AGENDA

Yoram Wind
Professor of Marketing
The Wharton School
University of Pennsylvania

INTRODUCTION

The concept of an organizational buying center as the relevant unit for analysis of organizational buying behavior, although appealing, has not received in the ten years since its introduction [165] the acceptance one would have expected. The purpose of this report is, therefore, to examine some of the issues involved in implementing the concept, assessing its viability, and discussing research priorities for the study of organizational buying centers. The evaluation of the concept and the suggested research priorities are intended to suggest some directions for further work in this important area.

MAJOR CONCEPTUAL ISSUES

The buying center was originally defined as "all the organizational members involved in the purchase decision" [165, 147]. This definition served primarily to draw attention to the difference between the more conventional focus on the buyer and the more accurate focus on *all* those individuals and groups involved in the organizational buying process. The concept of the buying center has been accepted in principle. Yet in practice it has been rarely applied beyond its intuitive utilization by salesmen who, in the course of their selling efforts, do frequently establish contacts with a number of organizational members and groups.

67

Most industrial marketing research studies center on members of the purchasing department and, only occasionally, pay lip service to the buying center concept by screening to interview the "major decision maker."

Two interrelated reasons may account for the lack of practical utilization of the concept:

1. definitional shortcomings due to the ambiguity of the original definition.
2. methodological difficulties in identifying the members of a buying center and assessing their roles and influence.

The remainder of this section is devoted to some of the major conceptual issues.

Direct vs. Indirect Involvement

The proper definition of involvement is not an obvious one. If one accepts the idea that *all* those "involved" should be included in the buying center, the center might include too many people who are only casually involved. The larger the number of center members, the harder it is to actually utilize the concept of a buying center. One would prefer, therefore, to include in the buying center only those individuals with major direct involvement in the given purchase decision.

But what should the definition of involvement be? One solution is to ask the organizational members "Who else is involved in the given purchase?" This direct approach, although feasible, places the burden of interpreting the term "involvement" on the respondents, and does not help us achieve a more rigorous and unambiguous definition of the term.

To help achieve a more explicit (and comparable) definition of involvement, one could further elaborate on the various aspects of the organizational buying decision process and ask the respondents to specify who is involved in which phase of the process—specification of need, determination of the budget, and selection of a vendor, for example.

Initial experience with this approach suggests that purchasing agents can, in most cases, identify the other organizational members involved in a given purchase decision. There is a high degree of consensus among the responses of purchasing agents and those of other "involved" organizational members. Purchasing agents are considerably less accurate, however, in assessing the degree of involvement and the importance of the various persons involved.

An explicit procedure for identifying the involved persons and assessing the degree of involvement is a necessary condition for any study of an organizational buying center. It is the researcher's responsibility to specify the minimum level of involvement which would qualify a person as a member of the buying center.

Role vs. People

In determining the composition of organizational buying centers, one has to determine whether the membership should be compiled by role (e.g., "purchasing agent," "controller," etc.) or specific persons (e.g., "Joe Smith"). In striving for guidelines for identifying the composition of buying centers under various buying situations, one would like to rely on organizational roles. Yet, individual idiosyncracies often necessitate deviation from the "role" prototype. From a practical point of view, it is important, therefore, to start by identifying the relevant roles but to allow for deviations from the role model by adding or deleting specific members in a manner based on their unique involvement.

Should Outsiders Be Included?

In determining the composition of the buying center, a key decision to be made is whether the buying center should be restricted to members of the buying organization or whether it can include outsiders. Outsiders would include members of other organizations such as the company's advertising agency and CPA firm. From a conceptual point of view, as long as the outsiders have a stake in the decision, there is no reason why they should be excluded. Yet, most of the current work on buying centers tends to limit the membership to members of the buying organization.

Single or Group Decision Maker?

A major question facing researchers concerned with the study of organizational buying centers is whether the buying center operates as a group making group decisions or as a single decision maker influenced by other members of the center.

The answer to this question is crucial. If the buying center operates as a group, the concepts and choice models of group decision making should be employed. On the other hand, if the buying decisions are being made by a single individual who is influenced by the other members of the center, individual choice models are relevant to the extent that they can assess and take into account the influence of the others [168].

Individual vs. Group Characteristics

To the extent that the buying center includes more than one member, any analysis of the buying center's characteristics cannot be limited to an examination of the characteristics of the individual members (age, sex, training, role, etc.) nor to the organizational characteristics (size, SIC category, degree of centralization, etc.). Rather, the analysis should include an explicit examination of the relevant *characteristics of the group,* i.e., the cohesiveness of the buying center, the leadership pattern, and the formal and informal network of communication among the center's members.

These group characteristics are difficult to identify and even harder to measure. Yet, they are important to our understanding.

Patterns of Formation and Change

Given that each purchase might require a unique buying center (because different persons are involved in the purchase of different products and services), an important and neglected issue is the pattern of formation and change of buying center composition and function.

From both marketing and procurement management points of view, it is important to understand the formal and informal ways in which buying centers are created and how their composition and formation change in relation to the products they buy and the purchase situations involved.[1] Understanding the pattern of formation and change (including the phasing out of a buying center) would provide better insight into the functioning of buying centers, and would supply the necessary inputs for better generalizing our knowledge of buying centers and classifying organizations according to the type of buying center they have.

Temporary vs. Permanent Buying Centers

The basic concept of a buying center suggests that it is a temporary organizational unit which may change in composition and function from one purchase situation to another. In this sense, at any given point of time an organization has as many buying centers as it has purchasing decisions to be made. Yet, given the varying importance and degree of newness of these decisions, most of the routine decisions can be performed by a permanent buying center more often than not composed of a single individual.

The newer, more unusual and more important the decision, the greater the likelihood that a buying center will be established to carry out the purchase decision.

The greater the number of products bought by a single buying center, the greater the tendency to turn it into a permanent unit. The extent to which a buying center receives a permanent or quasi permanent status depends on the organization's formal structure and the specific interrelationship between the buying centers and the purchasing department. The interrelationship between purchasing departments and buying centers has been surprisingly ignored despite the fact that purchasing agents do and should constitute the core of any buying center.

---

[1]The three buying situations most relevant in an explanation of organizational buying behavior are those identified in the BUYGRID model—the straight rebuy, modified rebuy, and new task [110].

71

Identification of the degree of permanency of any buying center, the conditions under which it tends to become a permanent unit, and the interrelationship between it and the formal organizational units for handling the purchasing functions should all be explicitly defined and assessed before any attempt is made to implement the buying center concept.

Single vs. Multiple Decisions

Since an understanding of organizational buying requires an understanding of the entire buying process and not just the final purchasing act, studies of buying centers should focus not only on the single decision of "to buy or not buy" but rather on the entire range of purchase decisions. These multiple decisions can include determination of the criteria to be employed, the relative importance of these criteria, the type of product to be purchased, its quantity, and its sources of supply.

Given that these multiple decisions are usually allocated among the various members of the buying center, any attempt at understanding the nature of the buying center should focus on the entire matrix of buying decisions by members of the buying center.

IDENTIFYING BUYING CENTER COMPOSITION
AND ASSESSING ITS FUNCTIONS

Accepting the concept of a buying center and defining its boundaries is only the first step. The next step is the development of an appropriate research design to identify its composition and assess its decision processes and functions.

In developing research designs one should decide between the analysis of available secondary sources (including, for example, salesmen's call reports) and the design of primary studies. Given the paucity of secondary sources, the more likely course is the design of specific research projects. These projects should be designed either as basic research projects aimed at a better understanding of the behavior of buying centers or as applied projects.

72

This latter case should include all market segmentation and positioning studies as well as all those studies aimed at the assessment of the market's response to the marketing strategies (such as pricing and promotion). The acceptance of the buying center concept suggests that the unit of analysis in all these studies should no longer be a single individual but rather the entire buying center.

Buying center based marketing studies should follow the principle of costing less than the expected value of the results. They should also follow the logic inherent in any market research study concerning the choice between cross sectional and longitudinal design, lab vs. real world studies, and survey vs. experimental vs. observational studies.

In addition, attention should be paid to the number of respondents and, when more than a single respondent is used, to the procedures utilized to reconcile any conflicting responses. Hence, an important aspect of any buying center study should be the explicit treatment, both at the data collection and analysis stages, of multi-person responses.

Cross Sectional vs. Longitudinal Designs

To date, most buying center studies have been cross sectional in nature. Yet, if one is to examine the formation and change of buying centers and their behavior (including the examination of concepts such as source loyalty, brand switching and changes in product positioning) serious consideration should be given to longitudinal designs.

Lab vs. Real World Studies

Although studies aimed at identifying the composition of organizational buying centers cannot rely on laboratory studies but should be based on studies conducted in the real world, numerous aspects of buying center behavior can be studied effectively in a laboratory setting. Most prominent among the issues that lend themselves to laboratory study are those aimed at the modeling and prediction of the buying center choice processes, including the buying center's responses to various marketing stimuli.

73

Observation vs. Survey vs. Experimentation

Although most of the current buying center studies rely on some survey procedures, one should not ignore two other important research designs: observation and experimentation.

Observation of the behavior of buying center members can be done both in a real world setting (via protocol procedures [165]) and in the laboratory. In both cases a variety of observational procedures can be employed ranging from video or audio-visual taping to content analysis of documents and communications among the members of the buying center.

Experiments in which the researcher can control and manipulate various inputs also seem to be an underutilized research technique.

Whether experimental or nonexperimental design is used, and whatever the degree of reliance on observation, one should always consider the advisability of using some unobtrusive measure to assess the response of the members of the buying center [146].

Questioning of One vs. Two or More Respondents

Whatever the research design employed, the major decision facing the researcher is the number of respondents per organization to be included. There is a great temptation to rely on a single respondent since it is by far the easiest and cheapest approach and there is no need to face the question of what to do with conflicting responses. Yet, given that a buying center is usually composed of more than a single member, it is the responsibility of the researcher to consider basing his study on more than a single respondent.

Whenever a study is based on a single respondent, the researcher faces the danger that the respondent's perceptions are not consistent with those of the other members of the center. In fact, in a recent study of buying centers for Scientific and Technical Information Services, lack of consensus between the two buying center respondents   ranged all the way from differences in perception of the importance of various center members to differences in the criteria used to evaluate alternative STI systems [166].

74

It is suggested that organizational buying studies be conducted on a minimum of two members of the buying center. Whenever possible, most members should be included. Analytical procedures should be developed for handling multiple respondents. Measures of congruence of responses should be employed and procedures should be designed to handle discrepant responses. For some initial efforts in this area, see Wind [164].

IS THE BUYING CENTER CONCEPT VIABLE?

Structured and unstructured observations of organizational buying behavior over the past ten years suggest to me that the concept of the buying center is a viable concept, central to the understanding of organizational buying behavior. As legal considerations become increasingly important to all business decisions and as creative buying of scarce resources continues to spell the difference between profit or loss, no marketing manager can ignore the fact that most buying decisions are not made by a single individual.

The relevance of the buying center concept is not limited to organizational buying. One could easily apply it to consumer behavior. In this context, it is not the housewife—the traditional purchasing agent for the family—nor even the entire family that would serve as the proper unit of analysis. It is the *family buying center* which is relevant. As in the organizational buying center, membership in a family buying center can vary from one purchase situation to another. Consider, for example, the purchase of cereals, which might involve the mother and children; the purchase of furniture, which might involve the husband and wife; or the purchase of a car, which might involve all the members of the family.

No general guidelines can, at this stage of our knowledge, contribute to a single "best" definition of a buying center, nor identify its members or measure its behavior. Each researcher, whether concerned with basic or applied research, should make his own choices among the various options. The concept itself does seem to this author to be clearly viable for both the study of organizational and family buying behavior.

75

RESEARCH PRIORITIES

The question now is "Where do we go from here?" Given that only a few organizational behavior studies have focused on the buying center, and that the various issues and options addressed in the earlier parts of this report have not been resolved, any progress on any of these issues will be of value in improving our understanding of the buying center.

The question of research priorities among the various conceptual and methodological issues often arises. In principle, no one should dictate to others what to study. Researchers should select those areas of research which are of personal interest and are of some value to the understanding of a given phenomenon. In this way cumulative research efforts on buying centers would eventually lead to a better understanding of the composition, function, and behavior of buying centers.

Whatever conceptual or methodological option is to be investigated, it is important, however, for the researcher to realize that it is only one of a number of possible options. It is to be hoped that research on buying centers will continue at both the basic research level as conducted at universities and at the applied level as a component of actual marketing strategies. It is the continuous interaction between the academic researcher and his industry-based counterpart that will contribute to our understanding of the buying center.

CONCLUSION

The above discussion reflects my own biases and is not intended to be exhaustive. It is hoped, however, that even this partial list of issues and methodological options would stimulate some interest in further examination of the composition and behavior of buying centers. It is my strong belief that improved understanding of buying centers is a crucial and necessary condition for a better understanding of organizational buying behavior. An understanding of the behavior of buying centers can only result from much work on the conceptual problems involved and the design and implementation of better procedures for data collection and analysis.

A METHODOLOGY FOR RESEARCH ON ORGANIZATIONAL BUYING BEHAVIOR

Bobby J. Calder
Northwestern University

Organizational buying behavior can be examined from a variety of perspectives. One is the individual decision-making of key organizational members, such as the purchasing agent. Another is that of aggregate relationships between organizations or organizational units. While both of these perspectives have been relatively neglected, there seems to be no barrier to utilizing either of them in marketing research. Guidance is available from any number of relevant studies on decision-making and on the economics and sociology of inter-organizational relations.

A third perspective is more complicated. From this point of view, organizational buying is seen in terms of the interaction among those individuals involved in any way with the purchasing decision. Studies of this interaction are not being conducted, apparently because of lack of methodology. This is unfortunate. At the same time that such research appears to be stalled, there is a growing awareness that organizational buying cannot in fact be understood solely in individual or aggregate terms. What we need most is information about how the activities of many individuals come together to shape purchasing decisions. The purpose of this paper is to suggest a methodology for conducting such research.

A number of researchers have grappled with the interaction among people involved in purchasing. Robinson, Faris, and Wind [110] sought to describe actual case histories of purchases in terms of interaction. They used flow charts showing the sequence of different activities and decision network diagrams. The latter display the persons involved in a purchase connected with each other over time by lines indicating the nature of the interaction. Despite its descriptive merits, however, the mapping approach appears to have had little utility for researchers. It does not in itself offer a methodology for conducting research.

The influential work of Webster and Wind [147] also may be seen as an attempt to characterize interaction. They have sought to identify the functional significance of interaction for organizational buying. They specify five functional roles as follows:

- buyers who have formal authority for contracting with suppliers
- influencers who affect decisions by providing information and criteria for making evaluations
- deciders who choose among alternatives
- users who work with the products and services purchased
- gatekeepers who control the flow of information to and from the buying center

These "roles" represent common patterns of behavior manifested by people in their interaction with other people concerned with purchasing. Although the five role descriptions are useful in pointing to the importance of various types of interaction, due to their *a priori* development, they have been much less useful in stimulating research.

Recently I have tried to draw together the threads from this previous work in order to create a conceptual approach that does suggest a methodology for organizational buying research [28]. This approach views interaction in structural terms.

There are three important elements to this structure. First, there is a set of people connected by informal, personal relationships. Second, there is a set of positions which are connected by formal authority relationships. Third, there is a set of tasks which are connected to form a flow of work throughout the organization.

In addition to the three relationships above, there are two others. One connects people with one or more positions, the other connects positions with one or more tasks. Fig. 1 shows one company's office products buying as a structure consisting of these three elements and five relationships. Note that the h's stand for people, p's for position, and t's for task elements. The curved lines indicate a personal friendship between h_4 and h_6. The dotted line indicates the assignment of people to positions. The solid lines indicate authority relationships for the p's and task precedence. The dashed lines indicate the relationships between positions and tasks. The figure was arrived at on the basis of unstructured interviews within the company. It represents a composite picture of the interaction entailed in purchasing office equipment.

Though the structural representation in Fig. 1 may seem very busy, it has some useful conceptual advantages. It captures the essence of each person's role in the purchasing process. A role entails the demands of the task, authority, and personal relationships that bear directly on a given position. There is no need to arbitrarily specify certain types of roles. The representation also captures decision network information of the sort contained in the Faris, Webster, and Wind mapping approach.

The first step in this methodology is to construct a structural representation for each of the organizational units in a sample. Ordinarily the representation should be specific to a given product decision class. This is accomplished by conducting unstructured interviews in each organization with the key people involved in the purchasing process.

A snowballing procedure is used within the organization to identify key personnel. Each respondent is asked to try to think of other people involved in purchasing. New names are entered on a master list and the individuals are interviewed if their role is not clear from other interviews. Part of these unstructured interviews must be devoted to a job analysis which fully specifies the task relationships. Calder [28] found that participants were able to provide information about other relationships, but they could not describe task units and task participation nearly as well. Participants find it hard to isolate what they are familiar with only as a flow of work over time. Job analysis can take the form of several specific techniques developed by industrial psychologists. Usually it will be sufficient simply to probe task issues more intensively in the unstructured interviews. This may well have to be supplemented, however, by some other technique, such as actual observation or diary records.

79

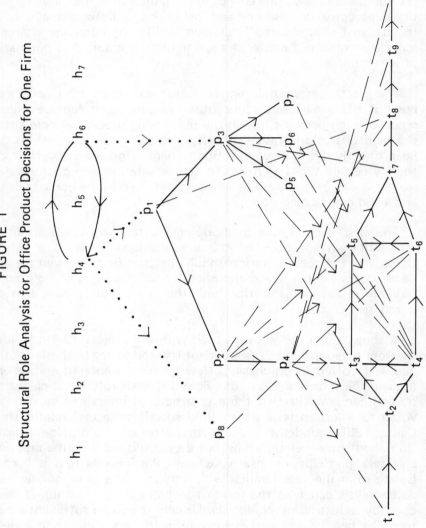

FIGURE 1

Structural Role Analysis for Office Product Decisions for One Firm

p_1 = Junior Officer

p_2 = Purchasing Agent

p_3 = Head of Printing Department

p_4 = Senior Buyer

p_5 = Technician

p_6 = Technician

p_7 = Technician

p_8 = Coordinator of Building Move

t_1 = Operating cost study

t_2 = Sales calls

t_3 = Maintenance problems

t_4 = Handling user complaints

t_5 = Meet with supplier

t_6 = Meet with competitive suppliers

t_7 = Technical evaluation of competitive suppliers

t_8 = Officer recommendation

t_9 = Order new equipment

t_{10} = Cancel present equipment

Once a complete structural representation is constructed, it must be validated. Respondents are reinterviewed. They are asked to comment on the accuracy of portions of the representation that reflect their own activities. The structural representation is then modified to incorporate these comments. Any inconsistencies between participants must also be resolved.

The proposed methodology is a two-stage one. The first stage yields a structural representation capturing the internal interaction of each organizational unit in the sample. In the second stage, every person identified as being involved in the purchasing process receives a structured, self-administered questionnaire. The questionnaire may measure any number of variables. The variables, in general, will concern the psychological perceptions and reactions of individual participants. For some variables, it may be appropriate to average the responses within organizational units to obtain aggregate measures (at the same level as the structural representation). Other aggregate measures can be obtained from objective records and archives. One objective, aggregate measure, for instance, would be the size of the entire organization of which the sampled organizational unit is a part.

Once both stages of the methodology have been completed, a general mode of analysis can be shaped. This analysis is summarized in Fig. 2. The structural representation is not a measurement in its entirely. Rather it is a simplification which allows measures to be defined on it. For example, one derived measure is simply the number of positions involved in buying, another is the presence or absence of different types of tasks (discussion meetings, for example). The advantage of the structural representation is that it does not bias the measures finally obtained. It is a method of discovering underlying patterns. Measures obtained directly from questions about specific features of interaction inevitably portray interaction in terms of those features. Measures derived from a structural representation are intended to allow the pattern of interaction to reveal itself.

The analysis of the data generated by this methodology has the objective (as shown in Fig. 2) of relating measures based on the structural representation to questionnaire responses and/or objective variables.

FIGURE 2

Summary of General Data Analysis

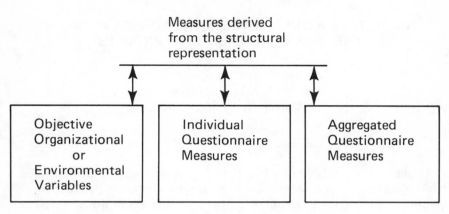

Measures derived
from the structural
representation

| Objective Organizational or Environmental Variables | Individual Questionnaire Measures | Aggregated Questionnaire Measures |

Without belaboring the possibilities, consider just one illustrative hypothesis which could be tested with this methodology: The greater the perceived technical product expertise (questionnaire data) of participants, the greater the number of interpersonal relationships in the structural representation interaction. Moreover, this association will be greater to the extent that the organization faces a competitive environment (an objective variable).

While this is perhaps a simple example, I would submit that it is just the kind of information we need about organizational buying. It is crucial, as a matter of marketing strategy, to understand what goes on inside the organization and how this is affected by other variables. If the hypothesis proved correct, perceived expertise and competition would signal the need to influence internal, informal communication.

AN ALTERNATIVE FRAMEWORK FOR EXAMINING
THE INDUSTRIAL BUYING PROCESS

Robert E. Spekman
University of Maryland

While marketing scholars [123, 147] acknowledge that the industrial purchasing process can be viewed as a dynamic interaction of several organizational members, there is little empirical research which attempts to examine the process from other than an individual level. For instance, researchers [82, 84, 161] have attempted to isolate the purchasing agent and have examined those variables which influence him.

With full recognition of the contribution made by these scholars, it is nonetheless true that in order to advance the study of industrial buying behavior and, specifically, the purchasing decision-making process, one can no longer isolate the purchasing agent and examine him as an individual acting alone. The purchasing process is a joint effort and any investigation must reflect that fact.

The goal, then, is to examine the purchasing agent *with respect to* the other organizational members who contribute to the purchasing decision. To accomplish such a task, the unit of analysis utilized in industrial buying behavior must include the entire group.

This report builds on the research of Webster and Wind [147] and others, and proposes an alternative framework for investigating the industrial buying process. The objective here is (1) to define and delimit that group responsible for purchasing related decisions, and (2) to present a methodology which permits the investigation of this joint decision-making process.

THE BUYING TASK GROUP

The concept of the buying task group (BTG) emerges from the buying center construct as developed by Robinson, Faris and Wind [110] and further refined by Webster and Wind [147]. The BTG captures the dynamics of the industrial buying process and its decision-making attributes.

The BTG is formally defined as the informal organizational subunit, composed of individuals from several functional departments, specifically charged with making purchasing related decisions relative to a particular commodity or class of commodities.

The BTG as an Informal Structure

The BTG can be juxtaposed with Duncan's [43] organizational decision unit which he defined as a "formally specified work group within the organization under a supervisor charged with a formally defined set of responsibilities directed toward the attainment of the goals of the organization. Decision-making *per se* may be centered in the formal leader and/or distributed to the various members of the specific unit" (p. 4).

Both constructs share major similarities. Both are structural subunits in which the focus centers on decision-making properties. In fact, the structural configuration of each is described in terms of its information processing potential. Yet, both constructs contain differences. Duncan's [43] decision unit is a formally defined entity which implies a functionally differentiated subunit [57] which can be located on an organizational chart. Its lines of communication, hierarchical levels, size, etc., are strictly prescribed according to organizational charters and accepted procedures. Such a structure implicitly stresses the vertical superior-subordinate relationships, and the notion of hierarchy of authority is a pervasive element.

Conversely, the BTG exemplifies Strauss's [129] conceptualization of lateral relationships within the buying process. The focus of the BTG is on the informal relationships which develop between the purchasing agent and those with whom he interacts during the purchasing decision-making process. This is not to say that hierarchical influences do not permeate the BTG. However, the BTG is not intricately bound to the formal organizational structure and depends, almost entirely, on the informal relationships that evolve during the purchasing process. Thus, it can be stated that the BTG defines a communication network in which the objective is making purchasing related decisions for a particular commodity or class of commodities.

The distinction between the formal and informal structure of these decision-making units can be further illustrated by comparing a purchasing department and a BTG. A purchasing department is a specified work group whose composition can be determined by examining an organization chart. One can easily locate the functional head of the purchasing department and would probably assess that this department is responsible for all purchasing related activity.

The BTG, however, is a more nebulous construct, reaching across functional boundaries whose composition can only be determined through investigation. Since the various members can conceivably share the same organizational level, the official hierarchy plays a minor role in the determination of the emerging relationships. Although a pattern of influence relationships will develop over time, this center of influence is not predetermined by the organizational chart.

Composition of the BTG

Consistent with the notions of Webster and Wind [147], the composition of the BTG is not constant over time. In fact, each purchasing context is thought to have unique characteristics which determine the nature of the BTG's composition. Some researchers have attempted to discriminate among purchasing contexts by the degree of routineness of the purchase [110, 147]; or by the degree of scarcity associated with the particular goods purchased [108]. The BTG's composition, however, is determined by factors basic to the workflow of the company. That is, business surveys [119, 162] suggest that the purchasing agent's degree of involvement, as well as the composition of the group involved in the purchase decision, varies with the type of commodity purchased. The composition of the BTG is commodity specific.

It would stand to reason that if the BTG is a decision-making structure and if the amount and kind of information required for a purchasing decision varies, the membership should also vary according to each individual's contribution. For example, within one company the information requirements for the purchase of steel and office stationary should differ to the point that different people would interact in different ways with respect to the purchase of each commodity.

This empirical distinction (i.e., commodity specificity) stems from the task differentiation which determines the structure of most purchasing departments. That is, the purchasing responsibilities within most purchasing departments are broken down into commodity classes so that a particular purchasing agent is responsible for a certain commodity or class of commodities. This task differentiation distinguishes one BTG from another and would theoretically account for the existence of several BTGs within one company, each with a potentially different structural configuration, degree of interaction, and information processing capability.

A METHODOLOGY FOR EXAMINING THE BTG

It is a relatively simple task to speak about the dynamics of the industrial purchasing process. Yet, attempting to address the issue in a given situation is far more difficult and is a primary reason for the lack of empirical research devoted to the industrial purchasing decision-making process. Webster and Wind's [147] conceptualization of the BTG entailed an approach in which they identified buying center members on the basis of what purpose each served (e.g., buyer, influencer, gatekeeper, decider, user). Operationally, however, such an approach is of little use to a researcher wishing to study the purchasing decision-making process. Specifically, Webster and Wind's notion of the generalized role relationships within the BTG does not accommodate a method for ascertaining the individual membership of the BTG, nor its decision-making potential.

The BTG as an Informal Communication Network

Since the BTG is an informally structured decision-making unit, knowledge of its communication patterns is crucial to the determination of its membership. Since the focus of the BTG concept centers on its cross-departmental composition, there are no formally defined lines of communication which can be traced from official organizational documents. Here, again, it is necessary to determine the communication networks of which the BTG is composed.

Membership in the BTG is empirically determined by the purchasing agent responsible for the particular commodity in question. Two important points, implied by that statement, have great bearing on BTG membership: (1) the importance of the purchasing agent in determining BTG membership; and (2) the importance of commodity specificity to the entire process. Operationally, the BTG is composed of those members of the organization with whom the purchasing agent states that he interacts in deciding on the purchase of a particular commodity. The purchasing agent becomes, therefore, the person about whom the BTG is structured. This is not intended to imply that the purchasing agent's position is central to the BTG in importance or status. His centrality merely serves to anchor the group's purchasing related responsibility to a particular commodity or class of commodities.

Having established the commodity in question, BTG membership is determined by following the communication network which is established by the purchasing agent with respect to that commodity. The BTG, then, exists as an informal communication network which does not derive its structural configuration from the normal organization *per se,* but rather from the regularized patterning of interpersonal communication flows. Rogers and Argarwala-Rogers [111] purport that this type of analysis permits a better understanding of the dynamics of organizational structural variables and is highly consistent with an open systems approach which emphasizes communication relationships.

A Macro-Sociological Approach—A Contingency Perspective

A macro-sociological approach, emanating from organizational theory, calls for an examination of the structural variables and relates this information to the interpersonal relations within the BTG under investigation. Basic to this approach are two important concepts: the ability to differentiate between communication patterns [55] ; and the capability to effectively solve problems [81]. Both concepts are closely aligned with the definition of the BTG as a decision-making entity and are highly consistent with the contingency view of organizational structure.

Simply, the contingency view seeks to understand the interrelationships within and among subsystems as well as between the organization and its environment. It also seeks to define patterns of relationships [71]. In this manner, it emphasizes the complex nature of the BTG and attempts to understand how the BTG operates under varying conditions and in specific circumstances. Duncan [43] and other contingency theorists have stated that organizational structure is the critical variable in determining the effectiveness or ineffectiveness of a decision unit's information processing potential.

For instance, a macro-sociological investigation of such structural variables as formalization and centralization can help explain (1) the degree to which the decision-making process within the BTG is regulated by strict rules and procedures; (2) the degree to which purchasing decisions are made by one member of the BTG or are shared by several; (3) the degree to which purchasing related activity in the BTG is differentiated; and (4) the degree to which communication channels within the BTG are restricted to rigidly defined paths. Such information indicates the information processing capabilities of the BTG and provides insights into the nature of its interpersonal relationships.

Since the BTG is a decision-making entity, the nature of the purchasing related information with which it must deal may vary over time and according to the specific purchase. That is, the degree of uncertainty associated with a purchasing decision is a function of the environment with which the BTG must contend with respect to its particular commodity. For instance, a period of material shortages and/or highly irregular price fluctuations would typify a fairly uncertain purchasing environment. Within that framework, one would assume that certain structural configurations of the BTG are more conducive to information processing than others and that the BTG would attempt to adapt its structural configuration so as to "match" the degree of environmental uncertainty with which it must contend. Specifically, a highly bureaucratized BTG structure restricts the flow of information to rigidly established channels; places limitations on the amount of information available to the BTG; and is more effective for dealing with more routinized, less uncertain purchasing environments [43, 79].

Take the opposite case of a BTG in which purchasing related activities and decisions are shared, communication flows are more informal, and the rules and procedures governing purchasing behavior are more flexible. This one will be more conducive to dealing with the more unusual and more uncertain purchasing related decisions.

It is possible to examine the BTG in interaction with its environment and from these results determine its decision-making potential. The macro-sociological approach then allows the researcher to draw inferences concerning the nature of the interpersonal relations within the BTG from an understanding of the BTG's particular structural configuration.

FACTORS INFLUENCING BUYING BEHAVIOR AND ACQUISITION MANAGEMENT IN R&D ORGANIZATIONS

Joseph P. Guiltinan
Associate Professor of Business Administration
University of Kentucky

INTRODUCTION

The objective of this report is to identify approaches for more effective management of the acquisition process for R&D systems. It analyzes the acquisition process in the National Aeronautics and Space Administration, using the Webster-Wind "buying center" concept as the basic framework for analysis, and suggests potential alternative mechanisms for improved acquisition management.

The observations and issues presented here are based on prior studies of contracting behavior in NASA and the Department of Defense [26, 50, 94, 97, 116, 118] and interviews with NASA Headquarters and field center personnel pursuant to developing case studies and other materials for the NASA Project Management Shared Experience Program and for the Low Cost Systems Office.[1]

While this paper focuses on R&D acquisition by NASA, it is similar in many ways to the processes used by other federal agencies doing R&D work.

Buyers in such agencies need to identify mechanisms for improving the acquisition decision process in order to attain certain goals.

---

[1] The author served as an AACSB Faculty Fellow with NASA from June 1975 to July 1976.

The "Buying Center" Concept

The Webster and Wind "buying center" concept is predicated on their finding that organizational decisions on purchasing involve more than one individual—especially for moderately complex and expensive items. Individuals in various parts of the organizations may be involved in the buying process in one or more of the following roles: user, influencer, decider, buyer, gatekeeper [147]. In this model, decisions made in the buying center are viewed as being influenced by four major factors: environmental, organizational, social and individual factors. After briefly examining these four factors in the context of NASA's R&D acquisition process, their influences will be evaluated and approaches to coping with each suggested.

ENVIRONMENTAL INFLUENCES

R&D acquisitions are characterized by a high degree of uncertainty regarding cost, the ability to maintain schedules, and the required level of new technology development.

Further, the generally high dollar value of such contracts—and the potential of such contracts for expanding an organization's expertise—means that they are often quite lucrative to suppliers, hence they will receive close scrutiny from the Congress, the General Accounting Office and the Office of Management and Budget.

The combination of uncertainty and of extensive government agency influences over budgets and contract awards results in a bidding procedure which is complex and lengthy.

Further, because of the levels of uncertainty and the significance of such projects, both to the contractor and to the acquiring agency, a highly interdependent relationship evolves between the contractor and the buying agency. Inter-organizational communications and conflicts regarding technical approaches, schedules, specifications, reimbursement terms, and reporting systems are frequent.

ORGANIZATIONAL INFLUENCES

The nature of buying tasks, organizational structure, and the technology relevant to buying an item or evaluating alternatives are some of the organizational influences on acquisition decisions.

Frequent changes in technical, schedule, and mission constraints contribute to the complexity and length of the R&D acquisition process. Due to this complexity and to the high visibility of the larger programs, many organizational units tend to become involved in influencing a buying center. In NASA, which is highly decentralized, R&D is funded and managed primarily through nine field offices, each being further divided into a variety of technical, business, and project offices. Many of these organizational components might be involved in the "buying center," each having its own concept of acquisition goals and tasks.

The organizational structure itself may exert conflicting influences on the acquisition process. NASA's matrix organization may be viewed as consisting of two major subsystems: The perceptual subsystem (composed of engineering specialists and procurement/financial analysts) acquires information, and defines, interrelates, and evaluates alternatives; the executive subsystem (headquarters program management and field center project management) translates inputs into decisions, strategies, and tactics [96]. The need for coordination mechanisms is further compounded by the fact that both subsystems at the field center level have headquarter counterparts who receive fewer communications from contractors and more from other federal agencies.

INTERPERSONAL AND INDIVIDUAL INFLUENCES

Interpersonal and individual influences will be considered jointly due to the difficulty in separating them in the observational/case study approach. These influences consist of role relationships, group interaction, non-task influences, and influencing tactics.

Some discussion of role relationships is implicit in such a discussion of organizational buying structure. Responsibilities are highly diffused, multiple buying goals and decisions are involved, and much more uncertainty exists regarding technology and cost. Therefore the influencer role is paramount. The project office tends to increase its relative dominance due to its closeness to day-to-day work, which enables it to monitor contractors much more easily than could be done at the headquarters level. Also, the lack of precise lines of

93

authority means that much acceptance of direction and much of the communication of activities and results to headquarters is a function of the willingness of project/center management.

Role relationships may also be affected by the tendency of matrix organized field centers to assign procurement personnel to project offices. This frequently leads to a change in allegiance and orientation of such personnel, who may become primarily responsive to the desires of the project manager (who has the power to reward them). Consequently, procurement offices in field centers tend to lose a good deal of influence. This results in the dominance of technical criteria over business criteria in decision-making.

Group processes with potential application to the buying center concept have recently been examined by Bagozzi [11]. Two theories appear applicable to certain R&D acquisition situations—"risky shift" theory and "social judgment" theory.

In the risky-shift phenomenon, decisions by groups have been demonstrated to be frequently more risky than decisions made by individuals. This may occur because individuals feel that a poor decision shared by the group protects against individual accountability, or because the organizational culture is risk-oriented and this orientation is part of role expectations.

Social judgment theory has been applied to problem-solving groups whose members differed on the appropriate policy to follow. Under certain conditions true group problem-solving may be replaced by informal bargaining.

Members of the buying group may be influenced by factors other than task demands. For example, contract negotiators or organizational units may unduly emphasize certain aspects of the decision making process in order to enhance their own status. Rule-evading, educational, and organizational-interactional tactics may be applied to influence acquisitions decisions. Communications to headquarters from field centers may be "selling oriented," a manager may be more project-centered than NASA-centered in decision-making, and the implications of required financial reports may not be communicated by the proper manager to headquarters.

IMPACT OF BUYING CENTER INFLUENCES

Viewed in terms of the impact on inter-organizational relationships, the influences cited above can lead to some significant constraints on NASA's ability to effectively maintain a balanced relationship with contractors. In particular, the following conditions can evolve too readily:

1. Contractors may be "encouraged" to submit "buy-in" bids in order to be "responsive" to field center estimates.
2. Expectations of various contractor performance criteria may vary among NASA components, both at a given point in time and over the life cycle of the product, to the extent that clear goal priorities are not maintained.
3. Technical changes are often made without adequate participation of the business system.
4. Cost growth (through changes or overruns) is often viewed as important only to the extent that additional funding is scarce.
5. There is a lack of coordinated strategy development within NASA because the inherent uncertainties of high technology projects are compounded by a variety of reviewing authorities and by intra-organizational conflict.

These conditions place serious constraints on cost-oriented acquisition management, particularly with regard to the manager-contractor relationship.

Two basic approaches can be used to alleviate such conditions. The "commercial business approach" (frequently advocated by contractors) places full responsibility for the entire process (beyond the definition of mission goals and performance requirements) in the hands of the contractor. This is generally an inadequate solution from the agency's point of view on most reasonably large projects because:

1. The agency will still bear responsibility for any poor performance in the eyes of the public and other branches of government.
2. Much of the technical expertise may reside in the agency.

3. Contractor technical and reliability testing motivations may be incompatible with the agency's cost objectives for a given project.

Accordingly, the development of schemes for improving the management process is essential to increasing the productivity of R&D dollars.

IMPROVING ACQUISITION MANAGEMENT

Several current management approaches appear to have potential value for dealing with the major influences presented by Webster and Wind. Each represents a potentially fruitful area to researchers studying organizational buying behavior.

Schemes for Managing Environmental Influences

Inter-organizational Strategy. Inter-organizational analysis has been applied to a number of organizations to analyze the power relationships in a network [17, 147]. Such an analysis permits the development of strategies designed to enhance an organization's ability to control environmental influences [54]. This enables buying organizations to develop acquisition strategies tailored to organizational resources—especially where long-term or contractual relationships with suppliers exist.

Contingency Management. The concept of "contingency management" is geared to planning and control in turbulent acquisition environments [94]. It suggests that organizations need to make decisions which consider not merely the current environment (of contractors, technology, costs, etc.) but also the impact of such decisions in terms of their influence on the future state of the environment so that maximum flexibility for coping with future conditions can be maintained.

What contingency management requires is the development of the ability to:

- avoid potential pitfalls
- predict likely contingencies

96

- develop plans for coping with likely contingencies
- implement contingency plans

While some supply, cost and technology forecasting is typically done by R&D buying agencies, the manner in which such information is processed and incorporated into acquisition planning and control activities has not been studied in depth in an actual buying situation to this author's knowledge.

Schemes for Managing Organizational Influences

Organizational Redesign. Where effective acquisition management is impeded by the nature of the buying task, by organizational structure problems, or by purchasing technology, attempts may be made to modify these factors through structural changes.

NASA introduced a Low Cost Systems Office to identify and implement cost-effective practices designed to reduce system acquisition costs by stressing cost goals of buying tasks and identifying new acquisition technologies. Such technologies include standardization of components and reduction of redundant specifications.

An alternative approach is the institution of an "acquisition executive" to serve as a focal point for clarifying buying goals, maintaining communications, and coordinating responsibilities for each major system acquisition [98].

Team Development. In situations where buying center membership remains largely intact over a period of time, it may be possible to view the center as an "acquisition team" and apply task-oriented group development approaches [14]. Potential benefits include improved clarification and adherence to group goals, roles, and decision-making processes; more efficient communications; reward structure clarification; and upgrading of the status of specific positions.

Schemes for Managing Interpersonal Influences

One very general set of schemes that may be useful falls under the label of "conflict management mechanisms." While this topic has received increasing attention [135] in the social sciences, a fully developed typology of mechanisms is still not available. However, a set of categories drawn from Stern [126, 127] appears sufficient for describing most mechanisms of this type.

Supraorganizational: In situations of perceived very high interdependence and interaction, conflicting organizations recognize their functional interdependence. However, they may vary in terms of their preference ordering among goals. Under such conditions, appropriate mechanisms include:

- joint participation in interdependent activities including goal setting
- third party mediation and conciliations
- independent commissions of inquiry.

Interpenetration: In situations of frequent interaction and high interdependence, more meaningful interaction can be achieved to reduce conflict through:

- exchange of persons programs
- establishment of permanent representatives in each other's groups
- ideological penetration via education/propaganda to improve trust and understanding of goals and values, to maintain positive activities which are consistent with the goals of the target system, to reduce ambiguity
- cooptation (absorption of elements of one group into the policy making activities of the other) to facilitate shared responsibility, and to utilize the specialized knowledge of individuals for adapting plans to local conditions.

Boundary Diplomacy: Where units are relatively independent, the process whereby personnel operating across organizational or group boundaries act as continual mediators to bring about compromise may be appropriate if such personnel have status in both groups.

Bargaining/Negotiation: Where low interdependence is perceived, this strategy may motivate resolution through a process

98

which legitimized heterogeneity of goals between groups, rather than encouraging adherence to a single goal.

Observations drawn from the author's experience with NASA suggest that all of these mechanisms are employed from time to time. However, arbitration from top management and other sources outside the buying center is relied on more than would be necessary if other mechanisms were effectively operating.

EXCHANGE AND DECISION PROCESSES
IN THE BUYING CENTER

Richard P. Bagozzi
University of California at Berkeley

One of the least understood and researched aspects of organizational buying is the buying center, defined as "all those individuals and groups who participate in the purchasing decision-making process, who share some common goals and the risks arising from the decisions" [142].

This report has two goals: First, to review a number of approaches that have been used to investigate small group phenomena such as the buying center. Second, to outline two new theories that can be used for studying the dynamics of the buying center—social judgment theory and Coleman's model of social action. Although these theories have not been explored in either the marketing or organizational behavior literatures, they offer a means for representing processes of exchange, power, and conflict in the buying center.

Given a group of individuals comprising the buying center, the research question addressed by this report is: How do the members of the buying center reach a joint decision in the face of diverse interests and differential control of events important to the group? Overall, the goal is to review and introduce theories and approaches that may help organization buying researchers, as well as businessmen, to better understand and manage the dynamics of the buying center.

Before turning to social judgment theory and the Coleman model, it will be useful to briefly review a number of alternative approaches that one might fruitfully employ. Most of these efforts have been

100

conducted in the organization behavior and social psychology literature on small group research.

LEADERSHIP AND DECISION MAKING

A number of researchers have focused on the role of leadership in
the decision making process. Much of the research has been descriptive and explanatory. Fielder and Meuwese [48], for example, conducted experiments investigating the relationships among leadership
influence, group structure (in terms of cohesiveness), and group performance. Four separate categories of groups were studied: military
tank crews, B-29 bomber crews, antiaircraft artillery crews, and a
number of ad hoc groups formed with university students.

In general, the results showed that leaders will influence the effectiveness of groups only if the groups are cohesive. For noncohesive
groups, it was impossible to determine whether the leaders did or did
not have influence. Cohesiveness was determined by sociometric
choice. Effectiveness was indirectly indicated by the correlation of
one's ability or achievement scores with the measure of group performance.

In another study designed to determine the dynamics of group
decision making, Jones et al. [70] investigated the use of covert
social influence strategies (e.g., ingratiation) which were loosely defined as "those witting and unwitting attempts to manage an impression so as to increase one's attractiveness to a particular other." Fifty
students participated as workers in three-party (one supervisor, two
workers) relationships and engaged in a game "designed to simulate
the features of a real business concern." Two independent variables
were manipulated. The first was *supervisory judgment.* It consisted
of an open-judgment condition where the subjects were led to believe
that the supervisor (an accomplice) had not made a decision concerning a series of problems to be solved (and thus, by implication, could
be influenced by the workers) and a closed-judgment condition
where the subjects thought the supervisor was "committed to a series
of problem solutions which he had worked out in advance."

The second was *supervisory values.* It consisted of a condition
where the supervisor was depicted as emphasizing the human side of

business—the spirit of cooperation, the importance of getting along with others, considerateness, understanding, accommodation, and solidarity (referred to as the SOL treatment), and an alternative condition where the supervisor was portrayed stressing "the quality and quantity of job performance above all else" (termed the PROD treatment).

The dependent variables included (1) measures of opinion conformity (as an ingratiation tactic) and (2) self description and ideal ratings as to (a) judgments of respect or admiration for personal strength and competence (respect items), (b) friendliness and approachability (affability items), and (c) ratings of the supervisor (flattery).

In general, the data supported the hypotheses. For the part of the experiment involving "important" issues, the subjects in the open-judgment conditions conformed more to SOL and less to PROD than did subjects in the closed conditions (F = 4.34, p < .05). Thus, the subjects employed conformity as an ingratiation tactic when given the opportunity.

The results with respect to the self-description portion of the experiment were mixed. Self-descriptions on traits connoting interpersonal warmth and congeniality were unaffected by the independent variables. However, with respect to the supervisory values manipulation, self-descriptions and ideal ratings on competence and personal power were more favorable in the PROD condition.

Subjects in the open conditions were more anxious to impress their supervisor with their competence than with their affability. Thus subjects seemed to use images of expertise as tactics of influence more than friendliness. Finally, the opportunity to use flattery was not used as a means of ingratiation.

In sum, it appears that workers in a relatively lower power position (e.g., buyers in the food industry) may use conformity and images of competence to influence a supervisor (e.g., a merchandise manager) rather than flattery, images of friendliness, or affability, provided the supervisor has not formed a decision prior to interaction.

In contrast to explanatory studies of leadership and decision making, a number of authors propose normative theories of leadership.

The path-goal model for leadership, for instance, emphasizes the role that a leader should take in specifying the connection between employee work behavior on the one hand and contingent rewards on the other (cf. [65]). More broadly, Vroom and Yetton [141] propose a normative model of leadership and decision making which prescribes the degree of involvement subordinates should be given based, in part, on characteristics of the organization and task environment, the perceived quality of the decision, the time required to make it, the degree to which the decision will be judged acceptable to subordinates, the information needed and available to the supervisor and subordinates (including cost considerations), and the anticipated conflict among subordinates, the degree of trust in subordinates. The author suggests that there are five possible decision processes that may be followed at various stages of a decision [141].

AI (autocratic I): You solve the problem or make the decision yourself, using information available to you at the time.

AII (autocratic II): You obtain the necessary information from your subordinates, then decide the solution to the problem yourself. You may or may not tell your subordinates what the problem is in getting the information from them. The role played by your subordinates in making the decision is clearly one of providing the necessary information to you, rather than generating or evaluating alternative solutions.

CI (consultative I): You share the problem with the relevant subordinates individually, getting their ideas and suggestions without bringing them together as a group. Then *you* make the decision, which may or may not reflect your subordinates' influence.

CII (consultative II): You share the problem with your subordinates as a group, obtaining their collective ideas and suggestions. Then you make the decision, which may or may not reflect your subordinates' influence.

GII (group II): You share the problem with your subordinates as a group. Together you generate and evaluate alternatives and attempt to reach agreement (consensus) on a solution. Your role is much like that of chairman. You do not try to influence the group to adopt "your" solution, and you are willing to accept and implement any solution which has the support of the entire group [141].

GROUP DECISION MAKING PROCESSES

In general, group decision making processes have been studied in one of two ways. One stream of research has investigated the effect of social influence on the decisions made by individuals in a group. The other research tradition has studied the determinants of risk taking and other behaviors of groups. Each of these is reviewed below, selecting representative studies.

In one of the early experiments to explicitly identify what aspects of groups actually induce conformity and changes in judgment in group members, Deutsch and Gerard [39] tested the impact of normative social influence and informational social influence in a modified version of the classic Asch [9] experiment.

Table 1 presents the five hypotheses and findings of Deutsch and Gerard [39]. In general, it can be seen that social and informational influence of the group can be significant, depending on whether one is a member of a group or not, whether one makes a self or public commitment to a position, or whether one is uncertain about the correctness of his or her judgment. These effects were in addition to the main effects of group membership which Asch [8] found (as can be determined by comparing the anonymous situation to the control group).

In another conformity study, Allen and Levine [5] investigated the effectiveness of several types of dissent as means of reducing conformity on both objective and subjective material. Test subjects were asked to make judgments on perceptual, information, and opinion items projected on a screen, and five experimental conditions were manipulated ranging from an extreme erroneous dissent condition to no dissent and veridical dissent conditions (the majority was always erroneous).

The dependent variables were the subjects' mean conformity scores on the three types of stimuli and the emotional reactions to group pressure for the subjects. The results of the study showed that "for visual perceptual items both the veridical dissent and extreme erroneous dissent conditions significantly reduced conformity. On opinion items, however, only the veridical dissent condition sig-

TABLE 1
Five Hypotheses of Normative and Informational Social Influences upon Individual Judgment
Deutsch and Gerard [39]

Hypothesis	Finding
1. Normative social influence upon individual judgments will be greater among individuals forming a group than among an aggregation of individuals who do not compose a group.	1. Strongly supported. The mean numbers of socially influenced errors in individual judgment among group members (12.47) differed from non-group members (5.92) significantly ($p = .001$ for the total of memory and visual tasks.
2. Normative social influence upon individual judgment will be reduced when the individual perceives that his judgment cannot be identified or, more generally, when the individual perceives no pressure to conform to the judgment of others.	2. Strongly supported. There was less social influence upon individual judgment in the anonymous as compared with the face-to-face situations. The p values for various conditions ranged from $p = .10$ to $p = .001$.
3. Normative social influence to conform to one's own judgment will reduce the impact of the normative social influence to conform to the judgment of others.	3. Strongly supported. For no commitment vs public commitment, F and A ($p = .001$), F or no commitment vs self commitment, F and A ($p = .001$); for self commitment vs public commitment, F and A ($p = .01$ and $p = $ n.s., respectively).
4. Normative social influence to conform to one's own judgment from another as well as from oneself, will be stronger than normative social influence from oneself.	4. The results are ambiguous. Although one version of self commitment reduced errors over no commitment, this version of self commitment was less effective than public commitment.
5. The more uncertain the individual is about the correctness of his judgment, the more likely he is to be susceptible to both normative and informational social influence in making his judgment.	5. Strongly supported. More errors were made in memory vs. visual treatments.

nificantly decreased conformity." The authors explain these findings as follows.

Persons hold strong expectations that group members will agree on matters of physical reality which are amenable to objective verification, such as length of lines. Only one objectively correct answer exists for visual discriminations, and a group's responses on such judgments are expected to be unanimous and correct. Lack of group consensus on visual items implies that the group's perception of physical reality is unreliable and therefore should not be taken as a basis for making perceptual judgments. Hence, in the extreme erroneous dissent condition nonconformity on visual items would result from the subject's rejecting the majority as an acceptable reference group and relying instead on his own perception of physical reality.

On opinion items other people's responses serve as the sole index of reality-social reality because objective bases for evaluation of the correctness or appropriateness of an answer do not exist (Festinger, 1954). Although visual items have only one objectively correct answer, for opinion items there are many equally reasonable and correct answers. Thus, lack of group consensus does not have the same implication for opinions as for visual judgments. Some degree of variability among group members is to be expected on subjective material, unlike the situation for visual items. Therefore, in spite of lack of unanimity on opinion items, the group is not rejected as a social referent. In the extreme erroneous dissent condition, conformity on opinions is perhaps not significantly reduced because the group is still employed as an index of social reality . . . .
. . . .
The mechanism primarily responsible for the effectiveness of veridical dissent on opinion items is apparently the emotional comfort of having a partner with whom to face the opposing group [5].

Thus, the effects of dissent and group pressure vary depending on the degree of objectivity of the issue comprising the judgment problem. In industrial buying settings, one might expect the influence of a dissenter on individuals in the buying center to vary depending on the interaction of the truth or falsity of the dissent with the degree of objectivity of the buying decision problem at hand. A veridical dissent appears to reduce conformity in both objective and subjective

106

situations, while an extreme erroneous dissent appears to reduce conformity only in objective situations.

A second research tradition has focused on the effects of group interaction on risk taking in decision making. In the typical experiment, test subjects are first asked to make individual decisions on a series of problems which allow for varying degrees of risk to be taken. Next, the individuals are placed in a group setting and are required to discuss the same problems and arrive at some group decision.

A number of studies over a wide spectrum of tasks and conditions have all produced the same result. There is a significant change in risk from the mean levels of risk of individuals before interaction to the mean levels for the groups. Invariably, the groups have tended to take higher risks than individuals take in what has come to be known as the "risky shift" studies [16, 142, 75]. In industrial buying, Levitt [83] and Sheth [122] have included perceived risk as important components of the purchasing decision.

Despite evidence indicating that groups tend to take higher risks than individuals, little is known why this is the case. One of the few studies investigating the dynamics of risk taking by groups has been performed by Teger and Pruitt [134]. These authors studied two competing theories for explaining the "risky shift." In the Wallach and Kogan [142] theory, it was proposed that the existence of the group produces a relative diffusion of responsibility such that, should failure occur, the individual members feel less personal blame and shift some of the blame to others. Wallach and Kogan [142] present indirect evidence indicating that it is some aspect of group discussion rather than information exchange with respect to preferences that produces the "risky shift." Further, they suggest that it is the "effective bonds formed in discussion" which specifically mediate the change in risk.

In an alternative account, Brown [23] posits a "value theory" consisting of two parts. Initially, before interacting with others, a person is thought to label decision problems as requiring either a "risky" or "cautious" approach based, in part, on cultural norms and past experience. Since some people will invariably be higher risk takers than others, interactions among group members will cause the revelation of discrepancies. Yet, because risk taking is a cultural value

107

in America, those who assumed initial low values of risk will feel pressure to change to higher levels, while those who were already high will not. Brown [23] suggests that the actual mechanisms producing the change are the exchange of information about initial decisions, the role of values for risk, and perhaps persuasive communication. This is in contrast to Wallach and Kogan's [142] "affective bond" hypothesis.

In their experiment, Teger and Pruitt [134] discovered that the risky shift emerged in groups that were not permitted to engage in a discussion but whose members could only exchange minimal information about their prior decisions. This finding would tend to refute Wallach and Kogan's claim that discussion and affective bonds are necessary and sufficient conditions for the risky shift [142] and at the same time lend some support to the value hypothesis of Brown [23].

For the discussion condition of their experiment, Teger and Pruitt [134] found an even greater shift in risk than in the information-exchange-only condition. This prediction is consistent with both theories. Teger and Pruitt [134] also found group size to be related to the extent of the risky shift.

"A minimal risky shift was found in groups of size three, a moderate shift in groups of size four, and a large shift in groups of size five," they report.

In terms of Brown's theory, such a finding would be explained by the fact that the larger the group the more the number of discrepancies and arguments arising. Similarly, in terms of Wallach and Kogan's theory, the larger the group the greater the opportunity for a spread in responsibility and accumulation of affect to develop. Finally, Teger and Pruitt [134] present indirect evidence indicating that the background of the individual and the nature of the problem task may also affect the risky shift, as one might expect from Brown's value theory.

COMMUNICATION NETWORK RESEARCH

Another line of inquiry that should prove useful for studying the dynamics of the buying center is the research into communication patterns of small groups. Bavelas [13] and Levitt [81], for example, found that communication structures of the wheel or star varieties performed faster, made less errors, and consumed less messages than circular patterns.

Mulder [93] investigated the effects of the wheel versus circle structure for communication and also the degree of centralization of the decision structure on the task performance of four-person groups.

With respect to the wheel and circle structures, a number of interesting findings resulted. In the early stages of problem solving, the circle structure produced faster solutions than the wheel structure, but this trend was reversed in the latter stages ($p = .01$). The difference between circle and wheel structures with respect to speed of solution on the fourth and fifth problem tasks (of the five problem situation) was not statistically significant.

In terms of performance quality, the circle structure produced less errors in the first two problem tasks, but by the fourth and fifth problem tasks, the wheel structure produced less errors ($p = .05$). The difference between circle and wheel with respect to performance errors on the last two problems was significant ($p = .05$). With respect to the number of communication messages sent, the wheel structure was progressively more efficient than the circle structure ($p = .01$). The difference in number of messages sent between the wheel and circle structures on the last problem task was significant ($p = .01$).

Mulder explained the difference between circle and wheel structures in terms of the development of centralized decision structures during the course of interaction (centralization was computed by a "decision centrality index" which depends on the content of communication). Centralized decision structures are characterized by a particular type of control achieved by a member of the group with respect to relaying information content. The more the control, the more the centralization. By analyzing the degree of centralization of groups on the final problem task, Mulder found that groups with a more centralized decision structure were faster, more accurate, and more efficient than the less centralized decision structure groups.

The results demonstrated that the decision structure was the important determinant of task performance, and this structure was relatively independent of the topological (wheel vs. circle) structure.

The results also indicated that centralized structures were more vulnerable in the early stages of problem solving in the sense of being relatively slower, more inaccurate, and less efficient.

For the buying center, one implication of this study is that centralized and/or wheel communication structures may be better decision networks than noncentralized or circular structures. Such a conclusion must be tempered by the fact that the experiments were performed under conditions where actors behaved in a rational manner according to the conditions of the game. If a member of the network were to function as a gatekeeper for selfish reasons which conflict with group goals, as shown in the buying study by Pettigrew [107], for example, then the conclusions of the study would not apply, and another theory would be required (such as the social influence model described below).

SOCIAL INFLUENCE PROCESSES

Another way to view the dynamics of the buying center is as a process of social influence where the actors attempt to affect the actions and decisions of each other through processes of give and take, threats and promises. There are at least three research traditions viewing behavior from this perspective: bargaining and negotiation, coalition formation and group effects, and social power approaches.

Bargaining and Negotiation

An extensive literature exists for viewing interpersonal behavior as a bargain or negotiation [113]. Although the approach appears to be most applicable to studying the buying center-vendor exchange, a number of insights can be gained by viewing relationships among buying center members as a bargaining process.

The social actors comprising the buying center may be thought to be engaged in multi-party relationships where some conflicts of interest exist along with a certain degree of mutual concerns. Bargaining occurs over aspects of the buying process (e.g., from whom to buy, how much to buy, under what terms, etc.), and the bargaining activities include various overt and covert attempts at influence.

Typically, bargaining will involve a number of suggestions or proposals made by one or more members followed by evaluation, discussion, and debate by the group. Invariably, the process will contain a considerable degree of give and take, persuasion, and even the coalition and power activities described below. Moreover, few bargaining relationships are devoid of processes of deference and demeanor; attempts to use one's authority; calls to various norms, rules, or other social conventions; or implicit or explicit alliances, deals, or understandings.

Rubin and Brown [113] review the literature supporting the impact that various structural, individual difference, and social influence variables have upon both bargaining behavior and the outcomes experienced by those engaged in these activities. In general, the following conclusions may be summarized:

Social Components of Bargaining Structure. Bargaining behavior has been shown to be affected by at least three social forces: the presence of audiences, the availability of third parties, and the number of participants involved. The presence of salient audiences motivates bargainers to seek positive, and avoid negative, evaluations. Audiences generate pressures toward loyalty, commitment, and advocacy of their preferred positions. Third parties function in a mediator role refereeing interactions, initiating agendas, restating issues and views, eliciting reactions, offering observations, pressuring parties to agree, and serving as buffers and even scapegoats. Finally, the number of parties involved in a bargaining setting determines the nature of emergent social patterns such as coalition formation, consensus processes, and status and other structural features of the group.

Physical Components of Bargaining Structure. The course and outcome of bargaining will depend, in part, on a number of physical constraints comprising the bargaining environment. In general, bargaining effectiveness will be reduced by barriers placed on verbal communication, face-to-face interaction, and (possibly) time limits for negotiating. Physical aspects such as the site or place for bargaining, the type of facilities available (e.g., size and shape of table), and so on may also affect bargaining behavior, but research appears to be sketchy and inconclusive.

Issue Components of Bargaining Structure. The nature of the issues existing between bargainers can shape bargaining behavior. Issues that result in zero sum outcomes (i.e., only one party influences or "wins" in an exchange) tend to induce dysfunctional competitive relations, intensify conflict, and promote the formation of intangible issues. Intangible issues (i.e., those involving one's public image, face saving, self-esteem) are likely to inhibit conflict resolution and thus result in lower joint outcomes for bargainers. The greater the number of issues, the greater the time required to reach agreement and the greater the pressures for differentiating among issues. Bargaining behavior and outcomes are usually enhanced when the number of issues, their sequence, format, abstractness, manner of presentation, and the display and arrangement of alternative solutions are consciously formulated [113].

Bargainers as Individuals. Bargaining behavior can be seen to vary with individual differences. Rubin and Brown [113] identify two broad categories of bargainers. The person high in interpersonal orientation (high IO) is "responsive to the interpersonal aspects of his relationship with the other. He is both interested in, and reactive to, variations in the other's behavior." The high IO who is *cooperative* "enters into the bargaining relationship with a posture that is both trusting and trustworthy." The high IO who is *competitive*, on the other hand, "enters into the bargaining relationship with an eye to taking advantage of the other." The person low in interpersonal orientation (low IO), in contrast, is characterized by a "nonresponsiveness to interpersonal aspects of his relationship with the other. His interest is neither in cooperating nor competing with the other, but rather in maximizing his own gain—pretty much regardless of how the other fares." The high IO and low IO distinctions can be used to summarize the impact of individual differences on bargaining behavior. Table 2 presents a capsule of the relevant research.

Interdependence. The nature of a bargaining relationship may be represented through three parameters: (1) bargainers' motivational orientation, known as MO (cooperative versus individualistic versus competitive); (2) the distribution of power in their relationship (equal versus unequal); and (3) bargainers' interpersonal orientation with respect to one another (high versus low). Rubin and Brown [113] present research supporting the following ten propositions:

112

- A cooperative MO tends to lead to more effective bargaining than an individualistic, and especially a competitive, MO.
- Equal power among bargainers tends to result in more effective bargaining than unequal power.

TABLE 2

Summary of Individual Differences and Their Impact on Bargaining Behavior

High IOs	Low IOs
Older children and college students	Young children
Blacks	Whites
Females	Males
Low risk-takers	High risk-takers
Externals	Internals
Abstract thinkers	Concrete thinkers
Persons high in needs for affiliation and power	Persons high in need for achievement
Cooperators (premeasured)	Competitors (premeasured)
Persons low in authoritarianism	Persons high in authoritarianism
Persons high in internationalism	Persons low in internationalism
Persons high in Machiavellianism	Persons low in Machiavellianism
"Normals" (remitted schizophrenics, nonparanoids, patients with good premorbid histories)	Abnormals (regressed schizophrenics, paranoids, patients with poor premorbid histories)

Summary of the Further Distinction of High IOs into Cooperative and Competitive

Cooperative High IOs	Competitive High IOs
Blacks (bargaining with blacks)	Blacks (bargaining with whites)
Persons high in need for affiliation	Persons high in need for power
Externals	Persons high in Machiavellianism
Abstract thinkers	
Cooperators (premeasured)	
Persons low in authoritarianism	
Persons high in internationalism	
Females	

SOURCE: [113, pp. 194-5].

- Under conditions of unequal relative power among bargainers, the party with high power tends to behave exploitatively, while the less powerful party tends to behave submissively, unless certain special conditions prevail.
- The smaller the discrepancy in bargainers' power, the more effectively they are likely to function.
- The smaller the total amount of power in the system, the more effectively bargainers are likely to function.
- Bargainers who are induced to be high in IO tend to function more effectively than those who are induced to be low in IO.
- Bargainers will tend to function most effectively when they share a cooperative MO and are of equal power, functioning least effectively when they share a competitive MO and are again of equal power.
- Bargainers will tend to function most effectively when they share a cooperative MO and are high in IO, functioning least effectively when they share a competitive MO and are again high in IO.
- Bargainers will tend to function most effectively when they are of equal power and high in IO, functioning least effectively when they are of unequal power and are again high in IO.
- Bargainers will tend to function most effectively when they share a cooperative MO, are of equal power, and are high in IO, functioning least effectively when they share a competitive MO, are again of equal power, and are again high in IO.

Social Influence and Influence Strategies. Bargaining will be affected by three aspects of social influence: the language of opening moves and gestures, the overall patterning of moves and counter moves, and the use of accompanying appeals and demands. Early moves and gestures set the rules and norms to be followed, the tone of trust and other cognitive and affective reactions to bargaining partners, and the starting points for give and take. The arrangement of offers and counteroffers conveys information in two important ways, "(1) When considered independent of the particular sequence in which they are patterned, moves present a picture of a bargainer's overall cooperativeness: the extent to which a mutually satisfactory agreement is of greater importance to him than one that maximizes own gain at the expense of (or without regard for) the other; (2) when analyzed in terms of the ways in which they are strung

114

together, moves describe the magnitude, rate, and timing with which concessions are made, and the extent to which these concessions are contingent upon the behavior of the other." Offers, counteroffers, and their patterning convey information as to one's preferences, intentions, and ability to exert influence. Finally, bargainers influence the course and outcomes of exchanges through the rewards and punishments they convey and the means they use to augment the communication of intentions (see the social power comments below).

Coalition and Other Group Effects

Members of the buying center also affect the nature and outcomes of their interactions through coalitions and similar processes of strategic affiliation and coalescence. The pioneering work in the study of coalition formation in three-party relationships has been conducted by Caplow [29, 30]. Caplow [29] suggested that parties in a triad will be motivated to enter coalitions based on the relative power differentials among the members. Table 3 summarizes Caplow's predictions for coalition formation of three-party groups, based on the relative magnitude of power for each person in the group.

In general, much of the research into coalition formation has been descriptive and predictive. Rubin and Brown [113] provide some hypotheses and review what little explanatory research there is. In summary, the authors conclude that "coalitions are especially likely to form in competitive, multiparty bargaining relationships when power (or other resources necessary for obtaining an outcome) is distributed, or perceived to be distributed, in such a way that one or more of the parties views himself as disadvantaged with respect to obtaining some outcome and does not consider it fruitless to join forces with another in pursuit of the outcome he seeks." Further, they maintain that coalitions will be inhibited "(1) when the combined initial weights or resources of the weaker parties are simply seen by them as insufficient to offset those of the more powerful parties. . . , (2) when a more powerful party effectively blocks the formation of alliances among weaker parties; and (3) when sources of external contention or conflict among would-be partners are of sufficient intensity that seemingly advantageous coalitions are avoided" [113, p. 71].

115

TABLE 3

Caplovian Coalition Predictions

Index of Relative Power for Each Member			Type of Power Relationship	Predicted Coalition	Character of Alliance
A	B	C			
1	1	1	All equal (A = B = C)	Any pair	Two parties pair to outweigh the third
3	2	2	One stronger (A > B; B = C; A < B + C)	BC	Two weaker parties pair to outweigh the stronger
1	2	2	One weaker (A < B; B = C)	AB or AC	Each stronger party seeks the weaker to outweigh other strong party
3	1	1	One all-powerful (A > B + C; B = C)	none	Coalition useless; weaker parties cannot outweigh stronger
4	3	2	All different (A > B > C; A < B + C)	AB or AC	Any coalition of two outweighs the third
4	2	1	All different (A > B > C; A > B + C)	none	Coalition useless; weaker parties cannot outweigh stronger

SOURCE: Rubin and Brown [113], p. 66, after Caplow [29].

Ofshe and Ofshe [100] have criticized coalition game research for failing to differentiate the choice process (selection of a coalition partner) from bargaining activities (especially the division of resources between partners), The authors present a theory based on individual decision making which explicitly provides for predictions of coalition formation.

Tedeschi, Schlenker, and Bonoma [133] propose a subjective expected utility analysis of coalition behavior which predicts whether a person will choose to enter a coalition and which partner will be chosen. Social psychological processes of prestige, interpersonal attraction, esteem, and status are modelled as determinants of these behaviors through their impact upon the probability of having one's choice of a coalition partner reciprocated, the utility of forming a coalition, the probability that the formed coalition will achieve its goal, and the utility of the goal.

Coalition behaviors have not been investigated in the context of the buying center. It is likely that coalitions would form in those buying center situations where decisions are made through joint debate and voting of the constitute members rather than in those cases where, say, a clear hierarchy of authority operates, or separation of responsibilities is the rule. In these instances, one might expect a considerable amount of covert and overt bargaining and exchange to occur among members of the buying center as they vie for control and form alliances. The social action model of Coleman (described below) provides a means for representing the outcome of bargaining and exchange among members of a group when these individuals are confronted with a joint task problem.

Social Power Approaches

A number of researchers view social behavior as a mutual influence process. Tedeschi, Schlenker, and Bonoma [132], for example, present a subjective expected utility theory of social influence where human interaction is represented as a process where actors attempt to change or modify a target's behavior. Influence is communicated through threats, promises, warnings, mendations, and the control of information and reinforcements. The source, in deciding how and what to communicate, and the target, in deciding whether to comply or not, both assess the probabilities and utilities associated with the contingencies in their respective situations.

The impact of communication is authenticated and augmented on the one hand, or deauthenticated and hampered on the other, through various aspects of the social relationship. Typically, processes of interpersonal attraction, prestige, esteem, status, and certain

117

message interactions serve to produce authentication or deauthentication of influence attempts. An impressive body of research exists supporting the many facets of the theory [132]. Except in the area of coalition behavior, however, the theory has not yet been applied extensively to relationships beyond that of the dyad.

OTHER APPROACHES

Nearly all of the approaches described above focus on the individual member of the group and his or her relationships to other members. A few studies have also investigated communication and structural patterns of small groups.

Industrial buying behavior may also be studied at a different level of analysis, i.e., at the level of the structure of the organization itself and its interactions with other organizations or aspects of its environment. At least two directions may be pursued. One approach would be to investigate the impact of certain macro variables on the behavior of the buying center. The independent variables might consist of organizational technology, size, complexity, centralization, formalization, or even environmental variables such as uncertainty. The dependent variables would be specific task or performance variables of the buying center such as time to reach a decision, quality of a decision (in terms of cost savings), etc. Such an approach requires that one look across organizations and buying centers in order to test specific relationships. Abell and Mathew [1] and Warner [145] present research employing this approach.

A second line of inquiry would be to investigate the relationships among organization structure; the structure of the buying center; operational features, such as specialization, standardization and authority patterns; and the organization's environment. Although beyond the scope of this paper, suggested research may be found in Woodward [170, 171], Thompson [137], Child [35], Duncan [43], Lawrence and Lorsch [79], and Hickson, et al. [62].

SOCIAL JUDGMENT THEORY

Social judgment theory (SJT) is a model concerned with human judgment processes in situations involving two or more persons.

Typically, the model is employed in settings where cognitive conflicts exist, in other words, where there is "disagreement among persons trying to reach consensus in the face of uncertainty" [108, 58]. This conflict is different from that envisioned by the bargaining or social influence theorists discussed above.

In the typical SJT study, two or more people interact so as to arrive at a joint judgment decision on some policy task. Conflict is created by either choosing and pairing subjects who differ in some way in the model they employ to reach decisions or else the subjects are trained prior to the encounter to use a particular model which differs from the model of the person with whom they will meet. The models used by subjects are usually called policies, and they may differ with respect to the forms of functions relating stimulus cues to judgments; the particular weighting of cues by subjects; certain organizing principles by which information is integrated; and consistency [59].

In the conflict encounter stage of SJT, the tasks for subjects are to study stimulus cues, make an individual judgment, communicate to the other, and decide on a joint decision. After this stage, the subjects are usually informed of the "correct" decision, and in some studies, the subjects are each asked to make a final individual judgment. The dependent variables in SJT are the individual judgments of the subjects in the group, their joint decision outcome, and the final (called covert) judgment of each individual. The policy models are usually represented through variants of the Brunswik lens model.

In general, a number of SJT findings may be summarized [21, 59]. First, evidence suggests that cognitive factors alone can create conflict even without the presence of differences in interests, emotional considerations, or motivational factors. Second, as the parties to a cognitive conflict interact, the structure of the conflict changes. In particular, numerous research efforts have found that there is little reduction in the magnitude of actual conflict over trials in SJT experiments. Rather the conflict in the initial stages is over systematic differences between policies, while conflict in the final stages is over disagreements caused by a lack of consistency in following particular policy rules. Brehmer [21] concludes in his review that studies show:

- that subjects do not resolve their overt judgmental differences

- that the failure to resolve overt differences is due to inconsistency rather than to inability to reduce the systematic differences in policy
- that the decrease in consistency can be accounted for in terms of how subjects change their policies as they interact
- that the concept of inconsistency has behavioral implications

One implication for managers in the buying center is that conflict can be reduced if rules and procedures, as well as criteria used by decision makers, are made explicit and communicated to co-members of the group.

A third broad finding in SJT studies is that conflict is affected by the problem itself. Research indicates that the consistency of a group member's policies is a direct function of the predictability of the task. The more uncertain the task, the greater the inconsistency. By implication, this would most likely entail more cognitive conflict. Similarly, greater inconsistency and conflict has been found to be associated with tasks requiring subjects to use multiple cues and non-linear relations between cue and criterion. Finally, it has been found that tasks with intercorrelated cues lead to less policy change than tasks with orthogonal cues, and also hide more fundamental differences in policies.

COLEMAN'S MODEL OF SOCIAL ACTION

Coleman [37] has developed a model of social action for determining the outcomes and degree of control social actors have in group decisions. Building on economic theory, the model assumes rational actions in the sense that people strive to maximize their utilities through exchanging control they have over events of interest to others. The fundamental data for the theory consists of (1) the matrix of control that each actor has for each event in a system of collective decisions, and (2) the matrix of interests each actor has in each event (which is based on a function of utility differences). Given these quantities, Coleman derives the value of each event, the power of each actor, the final control that each actor has over each event, and the outcome of each event (based on a particular probabilistic decision rule).

120

In order to illustrate the model, the following example, para-phrased from Coleman [37] may prove informative. The data required for an analysis of social action in Coleman's framework are of two kinds: a matrix, C, of control that j actors have over i events and a matrix, X, of interests (i.e., importances) that the j actors have in i events. Table 4 illustrates these two matrices for a group of eight actors and seven events. The entries in C, c_{ij}, indicate the fraction of control of event i lodged in actor j due to the social/political dynamics of the particular group or organization. For example, actor 2 controls .4 of event 2 and .7 of event 3.

TABLE 4

Control and Interest Matrices and Certain Relations Among Actors and Events

		C Actors									X Events							
		1	2	3	4	5	6	7	8		1	2	3	4	5	6	7	
	1	1	0	0	0	0	0	0	0	1	1	0	0	0	0	0	0	
	2	0	.4	.6	0	0	0	0	0	2	0	.8	.2	0	0	0	0	
	3	0	.7	.3	0	0	0	0	0	3	0	.5	.5	0	0	0	0	
Events	4	0	0	.4	.6	0	0	0	0	4	0	0	0	.7	0	.3	0	Actors
	5	0	0	.2	0	.2	.2	.2	.2	5	0	0	0	.3	.3	.3	.1	
	6	0	0	0	.2	.8	0	0	0	6	0	0	0	.3	.4	.3	0	
	7	0	0	0	0	0	0	1	0	7	0	0	0	0	0	0	1	
										8	0	0	0	0	1	0	0	

Z = XC								W = CX						
	1	2	3	4	5	6	7	8		1	2	3	4	5	6	7
1	1	0	0	0	0	0	0	0	1	1	0	0	0	0	0	0
2	0	.46	.54	0	0	0	0	0	2	0	.62	.38	0	0	0	0
3	0	.55	.45	0	0	0	0	0	3	0	.71	.29	0	0	0	0
4	0	0	.28	.48	.24	0	0	0	4	0	.20	.20	.42	0	.18	0
5	0	0	.18	.24	.30	.06	.16	.06	5	0	.10	.10	.12	.34	.12	.22
6	0	0	.20	.24	.32	.08	.08	.08	6	0	0	0	.38	.24	.30	.08
7	0	0	0	0	0	0	1	0	7	0	0	0	0	0	0	1
8	0	0	.2	0	.2	.2	.2	.2								

SOURCE: [37], p. 74.

The control that group members have over events may be estimated in a number of ways. In a group where decisions are made strictly by vote and each person has one vote, the amount of control for each person is simply 1/n where n is the size of the group. Often, however, the amount of control is not so easily calculated, and other methods must be used to determine the relative control actors have over events. This might entail an historical analysis of past decisions using achival data, an estimate of control using sociometric methods, judgments made by group members, a supervisor, or an observer, or some other method.

The entries in X, x_{ji}, represent the interest actor j has in event i. For example in Table 4, actor 6 has interests of .3, .4, and .3 in events 4, 5, and 6, respectively. Each x_{ij} entry measures the proportion of j's total interest in the system of Table 4 that is in event i. Interests may be calculated from an individual's stated utilities for outcomes. In particular, a utility of the outcome representing action on event i for actor j is depicted $u_{i_1 j}$, and the utility of the outcome representing no action is $u_{i_2 j}$; forming the difference yields the utility of an action relative to the status quo.

Next each actor's utility differences are scales "so that the sum of their absolute values over all events in the system equals 1.0" and aggregated over actors "only with explicit recognition of the implications for interpersonal comparison of utility" ([37], p. 71). This procedure yields *relative utility* differences, Y_{ji}:

$$Y_{ji} = \frac{u_{i_1 j} - u_{i_2 j}}{\sum_i | u_{i_1 j} - u_{i_2 j}|}$$

By scaling utility differences, Y_{ji}, so that

$$\sum_i |Y_{ji}| = 1 \quad,$$

the quantity $|Y_{ji}|$ may be interpreted as the interest of actor j in event i; i.e., x_{ji}.

Two important quantities can be calculated directly from C and X. Specifically, the product matrix Z = XC "represents a relation of control and dependence among actors." Its entries sum to 1 across each row, and a given row shows the distribution of control of j's interests among the various actors of the collectivity [37]. This is shown in Table 4. Each entry in Table 4 indicates the "fraction of one's total interest that one controls through event i." The quantities on the diagonal of Z, z_{jj}, represent "the fraction of [one's] interest that [one] controls, or the fraction that [one] controls the events that affect him."

Similarly, the off-diagonal quantities, z_{jk}, represent "the fraction of j's interest that is under the direct control of k." This may be described as actor k's amount of direct power over j, for it constitutes the degree to which j's interests depend upon the actions of actor k." For example, in Table 4, actor 7 has control over events of interest to actors 5, 6, and 8 as well as to himself. Moreover, actor 7 has interest only in events under his own control.

The second important quantity derived from Table 4 is matrix W = CX which represents the structure of relations among events. The diagonal entries in W, W_{ij}, depict the overall fraction of control over event i that is interested in i, while the off-diagonal values, W_{ik}, represent the fraction of control over i that is interested in k. In Table 4, for example, the matrix W shows that "those who control events 2 and 3 have interest only in these events, but that events 4 and 5 are partially controlled by an actor or actors with an interest in both events 2 and 3." Fig. 1 represents the relations among actors (matrix Z) and the relations among events (matrix W) in graphical form.

Coleman's model is essentially an economic model in that each actor is assumed to be driven by his interest to gain control over those events of most interest to him or her. This is done by exchanging "votes" based on the exchange rates and "prices" of events (outcomes). Each actor is assumed to behave according to a principle of maximizing control of events of interest to him.

Given only the matrix of control, C, the matrix of interests, X, and the economic assumptions (and a somewhat restrictive probabilistic decision role), Coleman's model provides for the calculation of the following quantities: the value of control over events; the power of actors; final control of each actor over each event; the outcome of each event; the increment in expected realization of interests due to one's own actions; increment in expected realization of

123

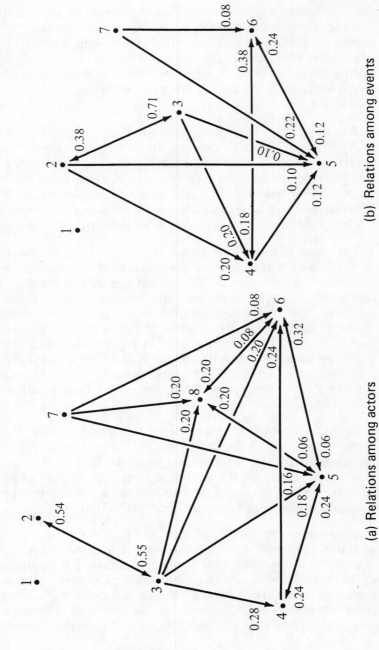

FIGURE 1

The Structure of Relations Among Actors and Events for a
Collectivity of 8 Actors and 7 Events

(a) Relations among actors

(b) Relations among events

124

interest due to external effects of actor k's action; expected realization of interest for actor j (i.e., the expected value of the collectivity to each individual); the total expected realization of interests for all actors; the directed power of the collectivity on each event; and the total power of the collectivity. Those quantities will not be discussed here [37].

THE ROLE OF THE PURCHASING AGENT
IN INDUSTRIAL INNOVATION

Mary Ellen Mogee
Policy Analyst

Alden S. Bean
Senior Policy Analyst
Division of Policy Research and Analysis
National Science Foundation

INTRODUCTION

An extensive literature exists on industrial purchasing agents and the industrial purchasing process, much of it aimed at increasing the effectiveness of corporate marketing efforts. In order to more effectively market to industrial firms, it is necessary to know who makes purchasing decisions, how responsibility is shared, what criteria are applied, what incentives are operating, and what the leverage points are for steering the decision toward a particular product.

This same information is needed by Federal policy-makers who desire to stimulate particular new technologies in industry. Not only does the *adoption* of new technology often require purchases. The *generation* of new or improved technological products frequently involves the purchase of components or materials that are new to the innovating firm. It has been suggested that most technology transfer in the United States occurs through the buying and selling of technological products between industrial firms [45]. For these reasons it is important to determine the role of purchasing and purchasing agents in processes of industrial innovation. This report will give the results of a preliminary search of the literatures on the role of purchasing agents in industrial innovation.

TRADITIONAL STUDIES OF PURCHASING AGENTS

Traditional studies of the "status" of purchasing agents provide information indirectly relevant to their roles in industrial innovation [6, 128]. By showing that negative perceptions of the activities of purchasing agents commonly exist, these studies cast doubt on the importance of purchasing agents in industrial innovation. The common perception of the purchase agent is as an "order writer," one who helps other departments achieve their goals and who is not generally regarded as an expert. The "really important" purchases are sometimes considered to be too important for purchasing.

The basic functions of the purchasing department are to negotiate prices and place orders on the best terms in accordance with requisitions, and to expedite orders and assure a smooth flow of supplies. Strauss [128] found, however, that many agents wish to expand beyond these functions. They feel they have important contributions to make by keeping management informed of developments in materials, sources, and price trends. Therefore, they want to be consulted before the requisition is drawn up.

Strauss presents a picture of running battles between purchase agents and engineers. Buyers tend to see engineers as quality-conscious—at the expense of cost—and as "gold-plating" their specifications. Engineers, on the other hand, see purchasing agents as overly cost-conscious and as seeking to interfere in the engineer's area of competence. The conflict is primarily over the purchasing agent's attempts to gain greater control over decisions of what to buy. He particularly wants more control over specifications. The purchasing agent wants specifications that are worded loosely enough that they do not limit his ability to find the lowest price, for this is one of the main criteria by which his job performance is evaluated. Partly in order to increase his control, and to prevent specifications being written that only one company can fill, the purchasing agent jealously guards his position as "gatekeeper" to the firm, and it is regarded as a cardinal sin for a salesman to go around the purchasing agent to talk with technical people or management.

It has been suggested that purchasing is "stronger and more highly regarded in low- to average-profit firms, while it is all but ignored in high-profit companies [6]. The reason for this is not clear, but it

127

may be related to another suggestion: that purchasing departments are most influential in situations where purchased parts account for a significant portion of total cost of the final product, that is, where there is relatively little value added. On the other hand, where value added by the manufacturing process is high relative to cost of purchased parts, purchasing departments may tend to be less important.[1] This suggestion is significant because high-technology industries, where rates of innovation are high, tend to have a high value added.

PURCHASING AGENTS IN THE INDUSTRIAL INNOVATION LITERATURE

Research on industrial generation and adoption of innovation has virtually ignored the role, if any, played by purchasing agents. No cases, surveys, or review articles could be located that mentioned them in any capacity. Some possible relevant work has been done on the adoption of industrial innovations, [33, 94], but these studies often focus solely on the role of the engineers involved.

The work on information sources and the flow of innovation processes [17, 45] points to the importance of groups positioned on the boundaries between organizations and their environments. The existence of "gatekeeper" roles has been suggested in regard to channeling technical information [4], and market-need information into the firm [69]. Purchasing agents appear to be a boundary group with access to important information about the firm's business environment that has been ignored by industrial innovation researchers to date. Studies are being funded by ETIP, however, on state and local government procurement that may produce relevant information.

One research project on the adoption of new products investigated the importance of various information sources at different stages of

---

[1] Based on personal conversation with E. Von Hippel who is currently involved in research on generation and sale of innovation in the scientific instrument industry. A supporting example is the importance of the purchasing department in the Ford Motor Company, where purchase costs account for two-thirds of costs of auto manufacture [20].

128

the adoption process in 40 industrial firms [105]. Information sources were classified as personal or impersonal. The process stages studied were defined as: "awareness" (first awareness of a new idea or an innovation); "interest" (firm seeks additional information about innovation); and "evaluation" (advantages and disadvantages are assessed).

. The most frequently mentioned personal source of information was personal selling, which was prominent in all three stages and constituted more than half of all mentions. The most frequently mentioned impersonal source was the price quotation and tooling proposal which is submitted by potential suppliers. This was not important in early stages but was the single most important source in "evaluation." The study also showed that the number and kinds of information sources utilized increase in the last (evaluation) stage. These findings imply that to the extent purchasing agents control entry of salesmen and bid proposals into the firm, they may exert considerable influence on the adoption of innovations.

SURVEY RESEARCH ON THE PURCHASING FUNCTION

More recent research has focused on the purchasing function as opposed to purchasing departments. This has been due to the increasing realization that:

> The industrial buying function is substantially more complex than it initially appears. It involves many people at all levels in a firm, often with vastly different views; it often is a protracted activity lasting many months; and it may even be influenced by factors that are largely unrelated to the quality and price of the product being sold. Hence, studies that tell about the activities of a purchasing agent or buyer tell only a small part of the story [151].

Surveys of the purchasing process have been made in both the United States [128] and Great Britain [25]. For the purposes of these surveys standard classifications of types of purchases (i.e., plant equipment, materials, and components) and stages in the process (i.e., initiating a project, determining kind of equipment/material/component, deciding on make or supplier) are used. These studies compare the importance of certain kinds of personnel in purchasing decisions across types of purchases and across industries.

A major finding from these surveys is that one pattern of influence holds for purchases of materials and components and another holds for plant equipment [24, 119]. In the first instance, research and engineering personnel are dominant in the decisions to initiate a project and to determine the type of product to be bought. A possible exception is when the purchase is initiated in order to take advantage of a new price differential, in which case purchasing dominates. Purchasing people dominate the selection of a specific supplier (although research and engineering remain important in this phase). In the case of purchases of plant equipment, this general pattern is modified by the increased role played by overall corporate planning and policy, operations, administration, and production engineering. Thus in this kind of purchase, which may be relatively costly and risky and which occurs less frequently, a broader range of considerations is brought to bear on the purchase decision.

At a more detailed level one finds that the initiation of purchases to contribute to a new product generally involves a broad range of interests, including design and development engineering, corporate management, research (materials) and operations (plant equipment). Purchases to change the firm's production processes are generally initiated by production engineering. Purchasing departments in these surveys appear to dominate such activities as surveying available makes and/or suppliers and selecting suppliers to bid. Technical people generally evaluate the submitted materials or components, then purchasing makes the final selection.

Reliance on the validity of the above findings must be tempered by the fact that the questionnaires on which the reports are based were filled in largely by engineers and research people. Only a few of the respondents were purchasing agents. Thus we would expect these findings to be biased in favor of a greater role for technical people.

CONCEPTUAL APPROACHES TO THE PURCHASING PROCESS

Webster and Wind [147] review many of the models of purchasing. Some models—such as "minimum price" or "lowest total cost"

130

models—attempt to explain or predict the purchase decision in terms of one factor assumed to be important in that decision. Others—such as "self aggrandizement" and "ego-enhancement" models—stress the personal factors that may affect a purchasing agent's decision. Complex models—such as the decision process model—are useful for descriptive purposes but have not been developed to the point of predictive accuracy. It will be useful for our purpose to go over some of the descriptive, complex models.

Webster [148] describes new product adoption decisions as a special case of purchase decisions which are especially important from the point of view of increased marketing efficiency. His framework includes buying motivation, amount of perceived risk, and information handling by the buying firm. The model was developed from a review of studies of industrial marketing, buying behavior, and diffusion of innovations. Regarding a company's promptness in adopting innovations, he says "Those firms which are first to adopt an innovation are those . . . for whom the innovation offers the largest relative advantage, as measured by expected incremental profit."

While this may be useful in a selection of marketing targets, it does not explain *how* profit motivation is integrated with perceived risk. Another deficiency is that it implies the existence of a single innovation as the focus of adoption decisions. This will be contrasted later with the view of purchasing as a problem solving process where the range of alternative solutions may be wide at first and narrowed through sequential steps.

Wind [163] applies the behavioral theory of the firm (as developed by Cyert and March) to the source selection decision and is able to explain several empirical findings about industrial purchasing in terms of four major concepts:

1. Quasi-resolution of conflict. Each group in the buying process has different goals. Engineering is concerned with performance; buyers want to minimize cost; production wants to assure timely delivery of all needed parts. The organization "lives" with this conflict through delegation and specialization in the various decisions that form the purchasing process. Acceptable level decision rules, rather than optimization rules

and sequential attention to goals, also help overcome the effect of this conflict.

2. Uncertainty avoidance. Uncertainty avoidance helps explain the widespread loyalty to existing suppliers and the unwillingness to use new suppliers unless necessary.

3. Problemistic search. This proposition states, "Any search carried out by the members of a buying center is stimulated by a problem and is directed toward finding a solution to that problem." Search follows the simplest route. Probably the vast majority of purchases involve no search, but are purely routine reorders. The author states:

> It was found that buyers, whenever engaged in search activities, start in their immediate neighborhood and initiate a search that is perceived to be the least expensive in terms of time and cost. Only if this search does not produce the desired outcome do they engage in a more "distant" and expensive search process.

4. Organizational learning. Learning in the form of experience entered all of the buying decisions studied by Wind. All buyers responded that in buying a new product they would use their standard search procedure, modified by their experience with similar products.

The empirical findings and the concepts underlying them imply an inertia in favor of the status quo that is overcome only by a significant problem that stimulates a search for new ways of doing things. Only when the costs of inaction become substantial will the firm face the uncertainty of innovation. The conflicting goals plus the only quasi-resolution of conflict mean that the purchase decision and responsibility will be fragmented and yet shared.

The framework developed by Robinson, Faris, and Wind [110] and applied by Brand [20] in Great Britain is probably the most relevant to our concern with the roles played by purchasing agents in industrial innovation. This framework views the purchasing process as a problem-solving process spread over time. Purchasing decisions are regarded as shared decisions subject to a variety of influences. Based on their study of three firms, Robinson *et al.,* concluded that type of product was not as important in determining the process as the situation regarding information and experience. They suggest three buying situations: the new task, modified rebuy, and straight rebuy.

A new task buying situation is characterized by the newness and complexity of the problem (little relevant experience), high information requirements, and important alternatives. Although it occurs relatively infrequently it is important because it sets the pattern for future purchases and products.

An example of a new task is the case in which a decision to start a new product line may require new types of equipment, parts, or materials. Not only does this category of buying situation appear to be closest to what one would expect to be involved in the *adoption* of innovations, it also includes situations where the purchase is necessary for the *production* of innovations.

The purchasing process is treated as a problem solving process with eight stages:

- The first phase is the anticipation or recognition of a problem of need. This phase entails both the realization that a problem exists, and the awareness that a solution may be possible through purchase.
- Second is the determination of the quality and characteristics of the needed item. This is usually done from within the firm, but outside sources can be helpful. At this point the process of narrowing down the solution has begun.
- Third, there is a specific description of the item needed.
- The fourth phase is a search for potential sources for this needed item.
- Fifth, these sources are examined, leading to a decision on how the item is to be purchased.
- In the sixth step, the supplier is selected.
- This is followed by the seventh phase, where the order routine is established.
- Finally, the eighth phase is an evaluation of performance feedback.

Based on Robinson *et al.,* and Brand, it is possible to generalize about the procurement process in new task situations: The problem

133

or need may arise externally (a forced reaction to competition from new technology or to new regulations) or internally (decision to reallocate resources to exploit a market opportunity or the need to update equipment).

Phases two, three and four are closely interwoven. For technical products, the using department may prepare performance specifications, or list ideal attributes which may be separate from considerations of cost and availability. In the purchase of technically complex or advanced items, user and supplier technical people may work closely together throughout the process. In involved cases, source selection may precede need determination. If good relations are formed with supplier technical people at an early stage, engineering selection of that supplier will be an important factor.

The search for suppliers varies but it is mainly in the hands of technical people. Purchasing may contribute lists of potential suppliers to be contacted. The assessment of the technical qualifications of suppliers or their product is the responsibility of the technical people.

After the basic technical problem has been solved, economic considerations enter the picture. It is at this point that the purchasing agent begins to share in the decision-making. By this time technical evaluations have narrowed the range of alternatives. If the purchasing agent has a choice between companies which are equally acceptable technically, he exerts great influence through his skills at appraising factors such as cost, delivery time, customer relations, and reputation.

After a new purchase is made, if regular re-purchase is continued, the emphasis shifts from what to buy and from whom, to getting the product at regular intervals to satisfy the needs of using departments. The straight rebuy is the most common situation. As repurchase becomes routine, responsibility is delegated from the chief purchasing agent to assistant purchasing agents, stock controllers, and purchasing department clerical staff. No technical questions are involved and no search is necessary.

On modified rebuys and straight rebuys the buyer is dominant. This is even true in cases where technical changes are involved, although the technical people will be consulted and may be involved in testing and liaison with the new supplier. Production personnel also must be convinced of the manufacturer's ability to manufacture and deliver a product that meets technical specifications.

In all of this it should be remembered that the purchasing process goes on within the environment of the firm. This imposes certain constraints. For example, technical plans for new products are guided by overall corporate planning and policy. Operating divisions plan their purchases and buyers operate within budget and inventory constraints.

To summarize, in new purchases technical personnel are most influential. They know what they want and generally how to bring it about, but they need information on the details in order to put their plans into form. They seek advice from colleagues in associated companies, noncommercial sources, and potential suppliers. In the early stages purchasing personnel play a largely information-providing role. In later stages, where factors of economy become predominant, the purchasing personnel take part more directly in the decision-making.

A Final Note

A notable characteristic of the purchasing process is that it differs from company to company and even within companies, especially in industries experiencing a rapid rate of technological and new product introduction. In part, the process variations can be explained by the significance of particular types of commodities to the purpose of the organization. For example, in one firm the quality of a new chemical material may be so critical that technical personnel will be heavily involved in the initial purchase decision, and once the quality is found satisfactory the purchasing agent probably will not risk changing suppliers. In a firm where the chemical's composition is not so critical, the purchasing agent may feel free to seek the best commercial terms with little risk of technical problems.

Conclusion

The purchasing agent plays an important gatekeeper role in industrial innovation but is not the principal decision maker in innovation processes that involve purchases. Although the sellers may attempt to contact and influence other parties in the adopting firm (e.g., top management or design engineers), they most often are required to go through the purchasing agent. Hence the purchasing agent partly determines the interplay of forces brought to bear on the initial and all subsequent phases of the innovation/purchase process.

Although in an innovative purchase situation corporate policy and technical factors may predominate, the purchasing agent makes a limited but critical contribution. He adds his own unique expertise— his knowledge of potential suppliers, their reliability for quality and delivery, and the price information without which an innovative product or process change could not come about. If the innovative purchase becomes a routine one, primary responsibility is shifted to the purchasing department. Thus, this department is one of the mechanisms for incorporating an innovation into the routine functioning of the organization.

Conflict between functional groups, as reported in earlier studies, is unavoidable given differing goals and backgrounds and the need for interaction between groups. To the extent that such conflict is not satisfactorily resolved, however, it could conceivably hamper innovative efforts. Moreover, to the extent that purchasing agents view themselves as mere "order writers" and do not see the possibility of making additional contributions to the firm, they may not keep abreast of or report on new or improved products or changes in price trends. This results in missed opportunities for innovation. Thus, higher status for the purchasing agent may promote him to a role which enhances his contribution to the buying process.

Implications

This brief review points to the importance of studying the "gatekeeper" role of purchasing agents in industrial innovation. The personal experiences of many salesmen attest to its existence, but purchasing agents are almost never mentioned in case studies of innovation. The purchasing agent appears to be one of relatively few points of contact between firms involved in technology transfer. Studies could fruitfully address the conditions under which the purchasing agent allows information to enter the organization and the

136

effects of this role on the rate and nature of technological innovation in the firm.

Another aspect of the purchasing agent's role that would bear study is the way in which the purchase selection factors of which the agent has special knowledge are integrated with technical and other factors in the innovation purchase decision. Do these factors enter early or late? Are they injected directly by the purchasing agent or indirectly through someone else? How important are they in determining the nature of the final "deal"?

A final implication, and one related to the long-range picture, concerns the possible effects of extreme formalization in the purchasing department on innovation in the firm. As a company or industry matures it is likely that purchasing departments become more "locked into" existing suppliers, commodities and ways of doing things, much as the production process itself becomes more standardized and locked into supporting and dependent systems [2]. Under such circumstances the purchasing department may be one more obstacle to radical product innovation. On the other hand, it may be conducive to incremental process innovations that are easily incorporated into the existing production process. A related topic concerns the role of purchased parts and their costs relative to value-added by manufacturing. This may also change over time due to experience in both supplier and user firms. Relating the Abernathy model of industrial innovation evolution to the role of the purchasing department also seems a fruitful area for inquiry.

RE-INVENTION: THE RESHAPING OF INNOVATIONS IN ADOPTION

Rekha Agarwala-Rogers
Research Scientist
Applied Communication Research

Since the writings of Ogburn [101] and Linton [87], most scholars of social change have made a distinction between *invention* and *innovation. Invention* is the process by which a new idea is created or developed, and *innovation* is the process of adopting an existing idea.[1] This distinction has led to thinking of the process of social change as consisting of three sequential steps: *invention; diffusion,* the process by which a new idea is communicated to the members of a social system; and *consequences,* the changes that occur within a system as the result of the adoption or rejection of the innovation.

Recently it has been acknowledged that an innovation often is not a fixed entity as it diffuses within a social system, and that in fact a new idea is frequently re-invented in the process of implementation by an adopter. The purpose of this article is to explain the concept of re-invention as it occurs.

LACK OF ATTENTION TO RE-INVENTION IN PAST RESEARCH

The common expression "re-inventing the wheel" suggests the apparent ubiquity with which a new idea is separately recreated each

---

[1] This definition applies to the *process* of innovation, not to be confused with innovation as an *object* (defined as "an idea, practice, or object perceived as new by an individual") [111].

time it is adopted. The phrase implies that re-invention occurs fairly often in a spontaneous and unplanned fashion, and that re-invention represents an unintended waste of resources through a duplication of activities.

Past concepts of innovation, diffusion, and adoption implied that an innovation, once invented, remained a fairly constant quality throughout the ensuing process of its diffusion. The new idea, it was thought, was reproduced in an identical way in each of the adopting units, and then implemented.

Certain anthropologists have noted that an innovation often undergoes *integration* (the process by which a new idea is incorporated into the ongoing operations of individuals in a social system), and *reinterpretation* (the process which occurs when the adopters re-create an innovation to suit their particular needs). Thus it was realized that an innovation may go through a gradual reshaping to fit the needs of individuals in a social system or organization. This process of gradually reshaping an innovation is the primary concern here.

The term *"re-invention"* is used to describe the process by which an innovation is changed in the process of adoption or implementation after its original development. It shall be maintained that, with a few exceptions, the process of re-invention has been almost entirely ignored.

Possible reasons for this lack of concern in past research will be explored, followed by a look at some possible reasons for re-invention. Finally, some research implications of re-invention will be considered.

Why has re-invention not been fully recognized in past research and writings about diffusion, nor in programs of change? The research literature on the diffusion of innovations gives the impression that adopter A uses an innovation in almost exactly the same fashion as the inventor or developer has envisioned it.

Downs and Mohr [42] have noted that "innovation has emerged over the last decade as possibly the most fashionable of social science areas." This popularity is perhaps explained by the fact that the

139

concept of innovation is associated with a very salient aspect of human behavior, one that conjures an image of improvement and betterment. This positive implication of "goodness" that is associated with the concept may have contributed to the oversight of the issue of re-invention. An innovation is popularly conceived of as good, therefore better than the existing idea that it is replacing.

Historically, diffusion research began with rural sociologists investigating the diffusion of agricultural innovations such as hybrid seed corn [115]. This particular innovation was almost universally advantageous to the Iowa farmers who adopted it. And hybrid corn could not be re-invented; it is a biological impossibility. Each year, a farmer must purchase a new supply of the seed. So modification of the genetic make-up *by the farmers* is not feasible. Naturally, corn breeders can modify a particular strain of corn to fit the needs of specific localities by creating various hybrid seeds [53]. The hybrid corn study by Ryan and Gross [115] has had a tremendous effect on 3,000 subsequent studies of the diffusion of innovations. Many of these innovations, unlike hybrid corn, could be (and probably were) re-invented, but diffusion scholars were intellectually blinded to this fact by their too-close following of the method and theory of the first study in the diffusion field. Past study of diffusion has generally stopped with the individual's *decision* to adopt an innovation; it has not really looked into the innovation's *implementation*, the process which begins with the decision to adopt an innovation, and continues through the steps involved in using the innovation, until it is institutionalized to the point at which the idea loses its newness and becomes an unrecognizable element in the adopting unit's ongoing operations [3].

Thus, the re-invention issue was simply not faced by diffusion researchers, who chose to simplify the reality they studied by treating the innovation as a constant. Had they pursued the innovation-process further, into acutal implementation by the adopters, they could hardly have ignored the fact that each implementation is at least somewhat idiosyncratic. But they stopped short of this realization.

The classical diffusion model assumed that all (or at least most) innovations were inherently "good" or "profitable" or that they had "relative advantage" over the existing practice they were replacing.

Such oversimplification has led to a pro-innovation bias [111, 140].
The hybrid corn study, as pointed out previously, helped set the tone
for later studies.

To past diffusion scholars, following the framework of the classical diffusion model, re-invention was an unwelcomed disturbance to
their main approach. For example, these investigators needed to
estimate the number of adopters of an innovation over time. To
explicitly recognize that the innovation might be taking varied forms
in its different adoptions was a discouraging complication to the
scholar.

WHY AND HOW RE-INVENTION OCCURS

Re-invention occurs when there is a lack of information about an
innovation at the stages of initiation and implementation of the innovation. Since innovations are not specified in operational terms, a
variety of usages among adopters can be found. The steps that constitute an innovation are not explicit enough and at times there is a
serious lack of information on how to get started. These and other
reasons lead us toward the re-invention of innovations at the initiation stage. The adopters, in the absence of relevant information, and
in the application setting of an innovation, decide to adopt the innovation and their decision is based on their understanding of the
innovation and circumstances. Such adoptions may not fulfill the
criterion envisioned by the inventor of the innovation.

The literature on implementation indicates that in the pure form
of adoption (whereby adopters implement the innovation in the
exact same fashion that the inventor or the change agency has envisioned and commissioned it), no re-invention occurs. There is *high
fidelity to the inventor's or sponsor's concept of the innovation.* The
literature also acknowledges the fact that a considerable degree of
re-invention takes place in the process of implementation. The
adopters adapt an innovation to fit their own circumstances, and
sometimes it is *mutual adaptation between the adopter and inventor
or the sponsoring agency.*

Thus, individuals come to the innovation adoption process with
different needs and problems. These needs and problems determine

the degree to which an innovation is re-invented. The degree of re-invention in turn, shapes the consequences of an innovation.

RE-INVENTION POSES PROBLEMS OF MEASUREMENT

Methodologically, re-invention is a messy issue because it poses problems of measurement for the researcher. The investigator, due to his/her quantitative approach, fails to recognize the issue of re-invention, an issue that is more qualitative than quantitative. Also the pressure to come up with precise answers in measurable terms makes investigators unwilling to delve into the issue of re-invention.

Change agencies discourage re-invention and they do not recognize that it exists. Their reluctance to deal with the issue arises from the problem of accounting for the rate of adoption among a given audience. Thus, they insist that if innovation is called "Innovation No. 3," it *is* "Innovation No. 3." They should recognize that re-invention exists and should take it into account whenever such acknowledgment would be beneficial.

RE-INVENTION POSES PROBLEMS OF RECOGNITION

Some of the early work in educational innovations indicates that credit for success goes to the inventor, but blame for failure is lodged with the teacher-adopter. Thus, in order to avoid such a predicament, the adopters re-invent an innovation and call it by a name of their choice. As one of the leaders in the field told me, "The Brownie points went to the innovators, not their imitators [49].

Utterback [140], summarizing 17 studies of individual technological innovations, noted that a majority of the innovations adopted by organizations are imported from other organizations. A large number of these innovations are from outside the industry. Out of these, 23 to 33 percent of the commercially successful products are wholly adopted from other firms. He further notes that these innovations are more likely to be process innovations than product innovations. A considerable amount of re-invention takes place in the process, more than in the final product.

142

Research Implications of Re-Invention

Researchers assume that when A2 says that he/she has adopted innovation No. 3, it has occurred. Instead we propose that there is a need to measure each of the elements in innovation:

$$\text{Inventor} \rightarrow A1 \rightarrow A2$$

We should look at which elements are adopted at each stage and with what effects. Is there synergy among the elements in their effects? Which element is most essential?

Any particular innovation is composed of a "package" of elements, and various combinations of such elements may take place in a given adoption. Perhaps changes must be adopted in addition to those included in the innovation itself. For example, it is essential for a farmer using hybrid seed corn to also use chemical fertilizer and a closer planting of the seed if the maximum yield is to be achieved. A diffusion study in Mississippi found many farmers who had adopted hybrid seed were not using fertilizer and closer planting, and thus were actually obtaining a *lower* yield than if they had not adopted hybrid corn [125].

The point here is that even though hybrid corn itself could not be re-invented by farmers, the context in which the innovation was used varied from farmer to farmer, so that the "innovation package" was re-invented by varying its components. Is there a critical mass of elements associated with an innovation which is necessary for its successful adoption? If yes, then there is a need for a clear-cut enumeration of these critical elements in order to measure the degree to which an innovation is adopted. A tentative determination of elements which are adopted and adapted—as an innovation moves from the center of origin to the adopters and subsequent adapters—would help determine the effects of innovation and its adoption in a given social system.

Do innovations in general tend to help the already innovative units or not? If so, then would adoption of innovations by the already innovative units widen the gap between the innovative and non-innovative units?

143

SUMMARY

Since the writings of Ogburn [101] and Linton [87], most scholars of social change have made a distinction between *invention* and *innovation*. *Re-invention* is the process by which an innovation is changed in the process of adoption or implementation. The common expression "re-inventing the wheel" suggests the apparent ubiquity with which a new idea is separately recreated in an adopting unit.

Past concepts of innovation, diffusion, and adoption implied that an innovation, once invented, remained a fairly constant quantity through the ensuing process of its diffusion. To past diffusion scholars, following the framework of the classical diffusion model, re-invention was an unwelcomed disturbance to their main approach.

Re-invention occurs when there is a lack of information about an innovation at the stages of initiation and implementation. Re-invention poses problems of measurement for research workers as well as for the change agency. Re-invention poses problems of recognition for the inventor and adopters of an innovation.

There is a need to measure each of the elements in innovation. We should look at which elements are adopted at each stage and with what effects.

REFERENCES

1. Abell, Peter and David Mathew. "The Task Analysis Framework in Organizational Analysis," in M. Warner, ed., *The Sociology of the Workplace*. London: Allen and Unwin, 1973.

2. Abernathy, W. J. and J. A. Utterback. "Innovation and the Evolving Structure of the Firm," unpublished papers, Harvard Univ., HBS 75-18, 1975.

3. Agarwala-Rogers, Rekha and Everett M. Rogers. "The Impact of EXPER SIM: The Diffusion and Implementation of a Teaching Innovation Among University Professors," paper presented at the American Educational Research Assn. Conference, San Francisco, 1976.

4. Allen, T. and S. Cohen. "Information Flow in an R&D Laboratory," *Administrative Science Quarterly,* 15 (Mar. 1969), 12-9.

5. Allen, Vernon L. and John M. Levine. "Social Support, Dissent, and Conformity," *Sociometry,* 31 (1968), 138-49.

6. Ammer, Dean S. "Is Your Purchasing Department a Good Buy?" *Harvard Business Review* (Mar./Apr. 1974), 36-159.

7. _____ . "Realistic Reciprocity," *Harvard Business Review* (Jan./Feb. 1962), 116-24.

8. Asch, S. E. "Effects of Group Pressure Upon the Modification and Distortion of Judgments," In H. Guetzkow, ed., *Groups, Leadership, and Men.* Pittsburgh: Carnegie Press, 1951.

9. _____ . "Studies of Independence and Conformity: I. A Minority of One Against a Unanimous Majority," *Psychological Monographs,* 70 (1956).

10. Bagozzi, Richard P. "Marketing as an Organized Behavioral System of Exchange," *Journal of Marketing,* 38 (Oct. 1974), 64-9.

11. _____ . "Exchange and Decision Processes in the Buying Center," paper presented at the American Marketing Assn. Workshop on Organizational Buying Behavior, Apr. 1976.

12. Bartels, Robert. "The Identity Crisis in Marketing," *Journal of Marketing,* 38 (Oct. 1974), 73-6.

13. Bavelas, A. "Communication Patterns in Task-Oriented Groups," in D. Cartwright and A. Zander, eds., *Group Dynamics.* New York: Row-Peterson, 1953.

14. Beckhard, R. "Optimizing Team-Building Efforts," *Journal of Contemporary Business,* Summer 1972.

15. Bell, Martin L. *Marketing: Concepts and Strategy.* New York: Houghton-Mifflin, 1972.

16. Bem, D. J., A. Wallach, and N. Kogan. "Group Decision Making Under Risk of Aversive Consequences," *Journal of Personality and Social Psychology*, 1 (1965), 453-60.

17. Benson, J. Kenneth. "The Inter-Organizational Network as a Political Economy," *Administrative Science Quarterly,* 20 (June 1975), 229-49.

18. Blain, R. R. "On Homan's Psychological Reductionism," *Sociological Inquiry,* 41 (Winter 1971), 3-18.

19. Blau, Peter M. "Parameters of Social Structure," *American Sociological Review,* 39 (Oct. 1974), 615-35.

20. Brand, G. *The Industrial Buying Decision.* London: Cassell/Associated Business Programmes, 1972.

21. Brehmer, Berndt. "Social Judgment Theory and the Analysis of Interpersonal Conflict," Umea Psychological Reports No. 87, Dept. of Psychology, Univ. of Umea, Sweden, 1975.

22. Brock, T. C. "Communicator-Recipient Similarity and Decision Change," *Journal of Personality and Social Psychology,* 1 (June 1965), 650-4.

23. Brown, Roger. *Social Psychology.* New York: The Free Press, 1965.

24. Buckner, Hugh. *How British Industry Buys.* London: Hutchinson and Co. of London, 1967.

25. Busch, P. and D. R. Wilson. "An Experimental Analysis of a Salesman's Expert and Referent Bases of Social Power in the Buyer-Seller Dyad," *Journal of Marketing Research,* 13 (Feb. 1976), 3-11.

26. Chapman, R. "Project Management in NASA," Natl. Aeronautics and Space Admin. SP-324, 1973.

27. Cardotte, E. R. and L. W. Stern. "A Process Model of Dyadic Inter-Organizational Relations," unpublished paper, Ohio State Univ., 1975.

28. Calder, B. "Structural Role Analysis of Organizational Buying: A Preliminary Investigation," paper presented at the Symposium on Consumer and Industrial Buying Behavior, Univ. of South Carolina, 1976.

29. Caplow, T. A. "A Theory of Coalitions in the Triad," *American Sociological Review,* 21 (1956), 489-93.

30. _____ . *Two Against One: Coalitions in Triads.* Englewood Cliffs, N.J.: Prentice-Hall, 1968.

31. Capon, N. "Persuasive Effects of Sales Messages Developed from Interaction Process Analysis," *Journal of Applied Psychology,* 60 (Apr. 1975), 238-44.

32. _____ , M. Holbrook, and M. Hulbert. "The Selling Process: A Review of Research," unpublished paper, Graduate School of Business, Columbia Univ., 1975.

33. Chakrabarti, A. "Some Concepts of Technology Transfer," *R&D Management* (Mar. 3, 1973), 111-20.

34. Champion, O. J. *The Sociology of Organizations.* New York: McGraw-Hill, 1975.

147

35. Child, John. "Organizational Structure, Environment and Performance: The Role of Strategic Choice," *Sociology,* 6 (1972), 1-22.

36. Cohen, Joel B. "An Interpersonal Orientation to the Study of Consumer Behavior," *Journal of Marketing Research,* 4 (Aug. 1967), 270-8.

37. Coleman, James S. *The Mathematics of Collective Action.* Chicago: Aldine, 1973.

38. Cyert, R. M. and J. G. March. *A Behavioral Theory of the Firm.* Englewood Cliffs, N.J.: Prentice-Hall, 1963.

39. Deutsch, Morton and Garold B. Gerard. "A Study of Normative and Informational Social Influences Upon Individual Judgment," *Journal of Abnormal and Social Psychology,* 51 (1955), 629-36.

40. Deutscher, L. *What We Say/What We Do.* Glenview, IL: Scott Foresman, 1973.

41. Douds, C. F. "State of the Art in the Study of Technology Transfer," *R&D Management,* 1 (1971), 129.

42. Downs, George W. and Lawrence B. Mohr. "Conceptual Issues in the Study of Innovation," paper presented at the American Political Science Assn. Conference, San Francisco, 1975.

43. Duncan, Robert B. "Characteristics of Organizational Environments and Perceived Environmental Uncertainty," *Administrative Science Quarterly,* 17 (Sept. 1972), 313-27.

44. Engel, James R., David T. Kollat, and Roger D. Blackwell. *Consumer Behavior,* 2nd ed. New York: Holt, Rinehart and Winston, Inc., 1973.

45. Ettlie, J. "A Longitudinal Study of Social Learning and the Technology Transfer Process," Ph.D. dissertation, Northwestern University, 1975.

46. Etzioni, E. *A Comparative Analysis of Organizations.* Glencoe, IL: Free Press, 1961.

47. Evans, F. B. "Selling as a Dyadic Relationship: A New Approach," *American Behavioral Scientist,* 6 (May 1963), 76-9.

48. Fiedler, Fred E. and W. A. T. Meuwese. "Leader's Contribution to Task Performance in Cohesive and Uncohesive Groups," *Journal of Abnormal and Social Psychology,* 67 (1963), 83-7.

49. Foshay, Arthur W. "Changes in Schools: An Insider's Look," paper presented at the National Seminar on the Diffusion of New Instructional Materials and Practices, Racine, WI, 1973.

50. Fox, J. *Arming America: How the U.S. Buys Weapons.* Boston: Harvard Univ. Grad. Schl. of Bus. Admin., 1974.

51. Gist, Ronald R. *Marketing and Society,* 2nd ed. New York: Dryden Press, 1974.

52. Goffman, Erving. *Frame Analysis: An Essay on the Organization of Experience.* Cambridge, MA: Harvard University Press, 1974.

53. Griliches, Zvi. "Hybrid Corn and the Economics of Innovation," *Science,* 132 (Mar. 1960), 275-80.

54. Guiltinan, J. "Contractor Relationships and Inter-organizational Strategies," in *NASA's R&D Acquisition Process,* NASA TMX 74314. Washington: Natl. Aeronautics and Space Admin., 1976.

55. Hage, J., M. Aiken, and C. Marrett. "Organization Structure and Communications," *American Sociological Review,* 36 (1971), 860-71.

56. Haines, G. "Process Models of Consumer Decision Making," paper presented at Consumer Affairs Workshop, Univ. of Rochester, 1972.

57. Hall, Richard. *Organizations: Structure and Process.* Englewood Cliffs, N.J.: Prentice-Hall, Inc., 1972.

58. Hammond, Kenneth R. "The Cognitive Conflict Paradigm," in L. Rappoport and D. A. Summers, eds., *Human Judgment and Social Interaction*, New York: Holt Rinehart and Winston, 1973.

59. ———— et al. "Social Judgment Theory," in M. F. Kaplan and S. Schwartz, eds., *Human Judgment and Decision Processes.* New York: John Wiley, 1975.

60. Harre, R. and P. F. Secord. *The Explanation of Social Behavior.* Totowa, N.J.: Littlefield, Adams, & Co., 1973.

61. Henle, M. *Documents of Gestalt Pyschology.* Berkeley: Univ. of California Press, 1961.

62. Hickson, D. J. et al. "A Strategic Contingencies Theory of Intraorganizational Power," *Administrative Science Quarterly,* 6 (1971), 216-29.

63. Homans, G. C. *Social Behavior: Its Elementary Forms.* New York: Harcourt Brace and World, Inc., 1961.

64. ————. *Social Behavior: Its Elementary Forms,* rev. ed. New York: Harcourt Brace and Jovanovich, 1974.

65. House, R. J. "A Path-goal Theory of Leader Effectiveness," *Administrative Science Quarterly,* 2 (1971), 321-39.

66. Howard, J. A. and J. N. Sheth. *The Theory of Buyer Behavior.* New York: John Wiley, 1969.

67. Huber, G. P. "Methods for Qualifying Subjective Probabilities and Multi-Attribute Utilities," *Decision Sciences,* 5 (1974), 430-58.

68. ————. "Multi-Attribute Utility Models: A Review of Field and Field-Like Studies," *Management Science,* 20 (June 1974), 1393-1402.

69. Huber, J. "Predicting Preferences on Experimental Bundles of Attributes: A Comparison of Models," *Journal of Marketing Research,* 12 (Aug. 1975), 290-7.

70. Jones, E. Edward et al. "Some Conditions Affecting the Use of Ingratiation to Influence Performance Evaluation," *Journal of Personality and Social Psychology,* 6 (1965), 613-25.

71. Kast, F. E. and J. E. Rosenzweig. "General Systems Theory: Applications for Organizational Management," *Journal of the Academy of Management,* 15 (1972), 447-68.

72. Kelly, P. et al., "Technological Innovation: A Critical Review of Current Knowledge," report to Natl. Science Foundation Office of National R&D Assessment, I, 237. Washington: Natl. Technical Information Service, 1975.

73. Kelman, H. C. "Process of Opinion Change," *Public Opinion Quarterly,* 25 (1961), 57-78.

74. Kessel, Colin. "Effects of Group Pressure and Commitment on Conflict, Adaptability, and Cognitive Change," in L. Rappoport and D. A. Summers, eds., *Human Judgment and Social Interaction.* New York: Holt, Rinehart and Winston, 1973.

75. Kogan, N. and M. A. Wallach. *Risk Taking: A Study in Cognition and Personality.* New York: Holt, Rinehart and Winston, 1964.

76. Kotler, Philip. "Marketing During Periods of Shortage," *Journal of Marketing,* 38 (July 1974), 20-9.

77. _____ . *Marketing for Nonprofit Organizations.* Englewood Cliffs: N.J.: Prentice-Hall, 1975.

78. Lavidge, R. J. and G. A. Steiner. "A Model for Predictive Measurements of Advertising Effectiveness," *Journal of Marketing,* 25 (Oct. 1961), 59-62.

79. Lawrence, Paul R. and Jan W. Lorsch. *Organization and Environment.* Homewood, IL: Richard D. Irwin, Inc., 1969.

80. Lazer, William. *Marketing Management: A Systems Perspective.* New York: John Wiley, 1971.

81. Leavitt, H. "Some Effects of Certain Communication Patterns on Group Performance," *Journal of Abnormal and Social Psychology,* 46 (1951), 38-40.

82. Lehmann, D. and J. O'Shaughnessy. "Difference in Attribute Importance for Different Industrial Purchases," *Journal of Marketing,* 38 (1974), 36-42.

83. Levitt, Theodore. "Communications and Industrial Selling." *Journal of Marketing,* 31 (Apr. 1967), 15-21.

84. _____ . "Industrial Purchasing Behavior: A Study of Communication Effects," unpublished paper, Harvard Univ. Grad. Schl. of Bus. Admin., 1965.

85. Levy, S. J. and G. Zaltman. *Marketing Society and Conflict.* Englewood Cliffs, N.J.: Prentice-Hall, 1975.

86. Liska, Allen E. "Emergent Issues in the Attitude-Behavior Consistency Controversy," *American Sociological Review,* 39 (Apr. 1974), 261-72.

87. Linton, Ralph. *The Study of Man.* New York: Appleton-Century-Crofts, 1936.

88. Lombard, G. F. *Behavior in A Selling Group.* Boston: Harvard Univ. Grad. Schl. of Bus. Admin., 1975.

89. Lutz, R. J. and P. Kakkar. "Situational Influence in Interpersonal Persuasion," *Proceedings of the Assn. for Consumer Research,* (Nov. 1975), 370-8.

90. Marrett, C. B. "On the Specification of Interorganizational Dimensions," *Sociology and Social Research,* 56 (Oct. 1971), 83-99.

91. Mathews, L. H., D. T. Wilson, and J. F. Monoky, Jr. "Bargaining Behavior in a Buyer-Seller Dyad," *Journal of Marketing Research,* 9 (Feb. 1972), 103-5.

92. Monoky, J. F., Jr., H. L. Mathews, and D. T. Wilson. "Information Source Preference by Industrial Buyers as a Function of

the Buying Situation," unpublished paper, Penn. State Univ. working series, 1975.

93. Mulder, Mauk. "Communication Structure, Decision Structure, and Group Performance," *Sociometry,* 23 (1960), 1-14.

94. Murphy, D., B. Baker, and D. Fisher. *Determinants of Project Success.* NGR 22-003-028, 1974.

95. Myers, R. and D. Marquis. *Successful Industrial Innovation.* Washington: Natl. Science Foundation, 1969.

96. Natl. Aeronautics and Space Admin. "A Study of NASA Source Evaluation Board Process Requirements Report of Task Team for Study of SEB Process," unpublished paper, 1975.

97. _____ . "Management Study of NASA Acquisition Process," unpublished paper, 1971.

98. Newell, A. and H. A. Simon. *Human Problem Solving.* Englewood Cliffs, N.J.: Prentice-Hall, 1972.

99. Office of Management and Budget. *Major Systems Acquisitions.* Washington: U.S. Govt. Printing Ofc., 1976.

100. Ofshe, Richard and S. Lynne Ofshe. "Choice Behavior in Coalition Games," *Behavioral Science,* 15 (1970), 337-49.

101. Ogburn, William F. *Social Change.* New York: Heubsch, 1922.

102. Olshavsky, R. W. "Customer-Salesman Interaction in Appliance Retailing," *Journal of Marketing Research,* 10 (May 1973), 208-12.

103. _____ . "Consumer Decision Making in Naturalistic Settings: Salesman-Prospect Interactions," *Proceedings of the Assn. of Consumer Research,* (Winter 1975), 379-81.

104. O'Shaughnessy, J. "Selling as an Interpersonal Influence Process," *Journal of Retailing,* 47 (Winter 1972), 32-46.

105. Ozanne, U. B. and G. A. Churchill. "Adoption Research: Information Source in the Industrial Purchasing Decision," *Journal of Marketing Research,* 8 (Aug. 1971), 322-8.

106. Pennington, A. L. "Customer-Salesman Bargaining Behavior in Retail Transactions," *Journal of Marketing Research,* 5 (Aug. 1968), 255-62.

107. Pettigrew, Andrew M. "The Industrial Purchasing Decision as a Political Process," *European Journal of Marketing,* 9 (1975), 4-19.

108. Rappoport, Leon and David A. Summers, eds. *Human Judgment and Social Interaction.* New York: Holt, Rinehart and Winston, 1973.

109. Rich, S. "The Impact of Materials Shortages on Purchasing Organizations," *Journal of Purchasing and Material Management,* 11 (1975), 13-7.

110. Robinson, P., C. Faris, and Y. Wind. *Industrial Buying and Creative Marketing.* Boston; Allyn and Bacon, 1967.

111. Rogers, E. and R. Agarwala-Rogers. *Communication in Organizations.* New York: The Free Press, 1976.

112. Rogers, Everett M. and Floyd Shoemaker. *Communication of Innovations.* New York: Free Press, 1971.

113. Rubin, Jeffry Z. and Bert R. Brown. *The Social Psychology of Bargaining and Negotiation.* New York: Academic Press, 1975.

114. Russell, Bertram. *The ABC of Relativity,* 3rd ed. New York: Mentor, 1958.

115. Ryan, Bryce and Neal C. Gross. "The Diffusion of Hybrid Seed Corn in Two Iowa Communities," *Rural Sociology,* 8 (Apr. 1943), 15-24.

116. Sayles, L. and M. Chandler. *Managing Large Systems: Organizations for the Future.* New York: Harper and Row, 1971.

117. Scheff, T. J. "Negotiating Reality: Nature on Power in the Assessment of Responsibility, *Social Problems,* 16 (Summer), 3-17.

118. Scherer, F. M. *The Weapons Acquisition Process: Economic Incentives.* Boston: Harvard Univ., Grad. Schl. of Bus. Admin., 1964.

119. Scientific American Inc. *How Industry Buys/1970.* New York: 1969.

120. Shapiro, S. J. "Marketing and Consumerism: Views on the Present and the Future," *Journal of Consumer Affairs,* 7 (Winter 1973), 173-8.

121. Segal, Erwin M. and E. Webb Stacy, Jr. "Rule-Governed Behavior as a Psychological Process," *American Psychologist,* 30 (May 1975), 541-52.

122. Sheth, J. N. "Buyer-Seller Interaction: A Framework," *Proceedings of the Assn. for Consumer Research,* (Winter 1975), 382-6.

123. _____ . "A Model of Industrial Buyer Behavior," *Journal of Marketing,* 37 (Oct. 1973), 50-6.

124. Silk, A. J. and H. L. Davis. "Interaction and Influence Processes in Personal Selling," *Sloan Management Review,* 13 (Winter 1972), 59-76.

125. Silverman, Leslie J. and Wilfred C. Bailey. "Trends in the Adoption of Recommended Farm Practices," Mississippi State College, *Bulletin 617,* 1961,

126. Stern, L. W. "Potential Conflict Management Mechanisms in Distribution Channels: An Inter-organizational Analysis," in D. N. Thompson, ed., *Contractural Marketing Systems.* Boston: D. C. Heath, 1971.

127. _____ . *Distribution Channels: Behavioral Dimensions.* New York: Houghton Mifflin, 1969.

128. Strauss, George. "Workflow Frictions, Interfunctional Rivalry, and Professionalism: A Case Study of Purchasing Agents," in A. H. Rubenstein and C. Haberstroh, eds., *Some Theories of Organization.* Homewood, IL.: Richard D. Irwin, Inc./Dorsey Press, 1966.

129. _____ . "Tactics of Lateral Relationships," *Administrative Science Quarterly,* 7 (1962), 161-86.

130. Strong, E. K. *The Psychology of Selling.* New York: McGraw-Hill, 1925.

131. Sullivan, Harry S. *The Interpersonal Theory of Psychiatry.* New York: Norton, 1953.

132. Tedeschi, J. T., Barry R. Schlenker, and Thomas V. Bonoma. "Cognitive Dissonance: Private Ratiocination or Public Spectacle?," *American Psychologist,* 26 (Aug. 1971), 685-95.

133. _____ . *Conflict, Power, and Games.* Chicago: Aldine, 1973.

134. Teger, Allan I. and Dean G. Pruitt. "Components of Group Risk Taking," *Journal of Experimental Social Psychology,* 3 (1967), 189-205.

135. Thamhain, H. and D. Wilemon. "Conflict Management in Project Life Cycles," *Sloan Management Review,* (Spring 1975), 31-50.

136. Thibaut, John W. and Harold H. Kelley. *The Social Psychology of Groups.* New York: John Wiley, 1959.

137. Thompson, James D. *Organizations in Action.* New York: McGraw-Hill, 1967.

138. Thompson, J. W. and W. W. Evans. "Behavioral Approach to Industrial Selling," *Harvard Business Review* (Mar.-Apr. 1969), 137-51.

139. Tosi, H. L. "The Effects of Expectation Levels and Role Concensus on the Buyer-Seller Dyad," *Journal of Business,* 39 (Oct. 1966).

140. Utterback, James M. "Innovation in Industry and the Diffusion of Technology," *Science,* 183 (May 1974), 620-6.

141. Vroom, Victor H. and Philip W. Yetton. *Leadership and Decision-Making.* Pittsburgh: Univ. of Pittsburgh Press, 1973.

142. Wallach, M. A. and N. Kogan. "The Roles of Information, Discussion, and Consensus in Group Risk Taking," *Journal of Experimental Social Psychology,* 1 (1965), 1-19.

143. Wallach, M. A., N. Kogan, and D. T. Bem. "Group Influence on Individual Risk Taking," *Journal of Abnormal and Social Psychology,* 65 (1962), 75-86.

144. Warren, R. "The Interorganizational Field as a Focus for Investigation," *Administrative Science Quarterly,* 20 (June 1975), 229-49.

145. Warner, M., ed. *The Sociology of the Workplace.* London: Allen and Unwin, 1973.

146. Webb, E. J. et al. *Unobtrusive Measures: Nonreactive Research in the Social Sciences.* Chicago: Rand McNally, 1966.

147. Webster, F. E. and Y. Wind. *Organizational Buying Behavior.* Englewood Cliffs, N.J.: Prentice-Hall, 1972.

148. Webster, F. E., Jr. "New Product Adoption in Industrial Markets: A Framework for Analysis," *Journal of Marketing,* 33 (July 1969), 35-9.

149. Webster, Murray. "Psychological Reductionism, Methodological Individualism and Large Scale Problems," *American Sociological Review,* 38 (Apr. 1973), 258-73.

150. Weigand, R. E. "Identifying Industrial Buying Responsibility," *Journal of Marketing Research,* 3 (Feb. 1966), 81-4.

151. _____ . "Why Studying the Purchasing Agent Is Not Enough," *Journal of Marketing,* 31 (Jan. 1968), 41-5.

152. Weston, John D. *The Molecular Biology of the Gene.* New York: Benjamin, 1965.

153. Whyte, W. F. *Human Relations in the Restaurant Industry.* New York: McGraw-Hill, 1948.

154. Willett, R. P. and A. Pennington. "Customer and the Salesman: The Anatomy of Choice and Influence in a Retailing Setting," *Proceedings of the American Marketing Assn.,* 1966, 598-616.

155. Wilson, D. T. "Organizational Buying: A Man and Machine Information Processing Approach," *Communication Research,* 2 (July 1975), 279-87.

156. _____ . "Dyadic Interaction: An Exchange Process," *Proceedings of the Assn. for Consumer Research,* 1975, 394-7.

157. _____ . "Models of Organizational Buying Behavior: Some Observations," in G. D. Hughes and M. L. Ray, eds., *Buying/Consumer Information Processing.* Chapel Hill: Univ. of North Carolina Press, 1974.

158. _____ and P. Bush. "A Theoretically Integrative Approach to the Study of Decision Making: An Empirical Analysis," *Proceedings of the Fifth Annual Conference, American Institute for Decision Sciences,* 1973.

159. _____ , H. L. Mathews, and J. F. Monoky, Jr. "The Effect of Perceived Similarity Upon Buyer-Seller Interaction: An Experimental Approach," *Journal of Marketing Research,* 9 (Feb. 1972), 103-5.

160. _____ and H. L. Mathews, "Impact of Management Information Systems Upon Purchasing Decision-Making," *Journal of Purchasing* (Feb. 1971), 48-56.

161. _____ . "Industrial Buyers' Decision-Making Styles," *Journal of Marketing Research,* 8 (Nov. 1971), 433-6.

162. _____ . "How Industry Buys," *Business Week,* 1967.

163. Wind, Y. "Applying the Behavioral Theory of the Firm to Industrial Buying Decisions," *The Economic and Business Bulletin,* 20 (Spring 1968), 22-8.

164. _____ . "Multiperson Influence and Usage Occasions as Determinants of Brand Choice," paper presented at the American Marketing Assn. Conference, 1975.

165. _____ . "The Determinants of Industrial Buyers' Behavior," in Patrick Robinson, C. Faris and Y. Wind, *Industrial Buying and Creative Marketing.* Boston: Allyn and Bacon, Inc., 1967.

166. _____ , J. F. Grashoff, and J. D. Goldhar. "Industrial Market Segmentation Under Conditions of Intraorganizational Heterogeneity," unpublished paper, Wharton School, Univ. of Pennsylvania, 1976.

167. Woodside, A. G. and J. W. Davenport, Jr. "The Effect of Salesman Similarity on Consumer Purchasing Behavior," *Journal of Marketing Research,* 11 (May 1974), 198-202.

168. _____ . "The Effect of Price and Salesman Expertise on Customer Purchasing Behavior," *Journal of Business,* 1975.

169. _____ and R. W. Pitts. "Consumer Response to Alternative Selling Strategies: A Field Experiment," unpublished paper, Univ. of South Carolina, 1975.

170. Woodward, Joan. *Industrial Organization: Theory and Practice.* Oxford: Oxford Univ. Press, 1965.

171. _____ . *Industrial Organization: Behaviour and Control.* Oxford: Oxford Univ. Press, 1970.

172. Zaltman, Gerald, Robert Duncan, and Johnny Holbek. *Innovations and Organizations.* New York: Wiley Interscience, 1973.

173. _____ and Thomas V. Bonoma. "Organizational Buying Behavior: Hypotheses and Directions," *Industrial Marketing Management,* 6 (Feb. 1977), 53-60.